PLACEMENT DIARIES

KNOW TO TACKLE THE CHALLENGES IN YOUR PLACEMENT JOURNEY.

ABHISHEK KUMAR SINGH

To my parents, Manoj Kumar Singh and Seema Singh, Wife, Bineeta Kumari and my brother, Vivek Kumar Singh: Thank you for your unwavering support and encouragement that made this book possible. I hope this work brings you joy rather than nostalgia.

To my readers: May you find inspiration and connection in these pages. Wishing you an enriching journey through this book. Happy reading!

Contents

Contents

Updated Version Of "placement Diares"

We're excited to announce that "Placement Diaries" has been updated with a new cover and additional chapters! This latest edition includes the final chapter, which was missing in the previous version, and offers a more detailed account of the author's transition from private sector employment to a government position.

In this updated edition, you'll find a comprehensive narrative of the author's journey through multiple government exams and his experiences in the corporate world. We invite you to explore these new insights and share your reviews with us. Your feedback is greatly appreciated!

Foreword

Writing my own book has always been a cherished dream, one that gained urgency with my passion for writing despite not yet having a published work. I'm deeply grateful to Notionpress.com for providing the platform to make this dream a reality.

Growing up in a Tier 3 city, often regarded as a "village," I faced limited exposure to English, both in speaking and writing. The lack of emphasis on grammar at school made me appreciate the value of writing more deeply, especially as board exams pushed me to improve my skills. This book chronicles my journey from those humble beginnings to crafting a motivational work designed to inspire others who may lack confidence but aspire to succeed.

If my story can resonate with you, I believe you can achieve your dreams as well. Please read, share your reviews, and feel free to point out any errors for correction.

Preface

The aptitude exam is often the first major hurdle for students aspiring to secure placements with recruiting companies. The hype surrounding these exams is usually fueled by seniors or classmates, making them seem daunting. The question that looms large in our minds is often, "Can I clear it?" Compounding this anxiety is the challenge of attending pool drives, which require additional financial expenditure and can be particularly stressful if they occur outside your college. Failing an aptitude exam during such drives can leave you in a tough situation, especially if it means having to explain your financial strain to your parents.

Another common dilemma faced by freshers is whether to focus on preparing for the GATE exam, placement interviews, or aptitude tests. Balancing preparation for both can be overwhelming, leading to indecision and stress. I personally struggled with this balance, often finding myself in a tough spot trying to manage time and preparation for both GATE and placements.

The more you struggle to secure a job, the more you face criticism from those around you, and it can become increasingly uncomfortable to ask your parents for money to attend additional drives. This book delves into these challenges and offers guidance based on my experiences. It aims to address your concerns and help alleviate the fear of interviews. While this book won't teach you the specifics of preparing for campus interviews, it will provide valuable insights into the process, the difficulties involved, and strategies for overcoming them.

Part 1: Navigating Campus Drives

This section explores the intense pressure and emotional strain of campus drives and pool drives, offering practical advice and personal anecdotes to help you manage these challenges effectively.

Part 2: Transitioning to the Corporate World

"A Way to Corporate World" is the second part of this book, detailing the sudden and drastic changes that come with stepping into a corporate environment. It covers the unexpected shifts in routine and behavior, and how to adapt to a professional setting. You'll learn about my personal journey from working at L&T to preparing for government exams, and how I navigated this transition to find a sense of personal fulfillment.

Part 3: Preparing for Government Exams

In the final part of this book, I share my experiences of resuming preparation for government exams after resigning from my corporate job. Having been away from formal study for nearly 2.5 years, rekindling my study habits was a significant challenge. I recount the difficulties of re-establishing a study routine and the skepticism I faced from those around me.

I hope this book helps you understand and navigate the complexities of transitioning to a corporate career and preparing for competitive exams. Fasten your seatbelt, and join me on this roller coaster ride.

Remember, the challenges might seem overwhelming, but they are not insurmountable!

Abhishek Kumar Singh

Mechanical Engineer, NIT Manipur

Formerly Placed at L&T ECC

Acknowledgements

I am deeply grateful to Notionpress.com for the incredible opportunity to publish my first book through their platform. Words cannot fully express my gratitude.

My love for writing began in 9th grade, despite initially struggling with English. Two key teachers, **Javed Arshad Sir** and **Kamal Pokharel Sir**, were instrumental in changing my perspective. Javed Sir's insistence on writing essays and Kamal Sir's English instruction ignited my passion for writing. Additionally, my friend **Mohit Ranjan's** skill in poetry inspired me to develop my own writing habits.

Throughout my education and career, I seized every opportunity to write—whether on Facebook, in diaries, or for newspapers. This persistence led me to finally fulfill my dream of writing a book. I hope readers find this book relatable and helpful in navigating job search challenges, and that it keeps you engaged through to the final chapter.

Thank you to all who purchased this book. I trust it will offer you motivation and insight.

Thanks,

Abhishek Kumar Singh

Prologue

He dreams of securing a position in a prestigious multinational corporation, fulfilling his family's aspirations, and becoming a financial pillar for his parents. However, until his third year of Engineering, he hadn't invested much time in his studies. With a list of dream companies in mind, he now faces a daunting challenge: mastering the entire Engineering syllabus and the fundamentals of Aptitude before his fourth year begins and the placement season kicks off.

Observing his seniors, he notices that placement statistics for his branch are less than encouraging. This concern intensifies as he learns that many seniors were still unplaced just two months before their final semester ended. Such realities can be unsettling for someone on the brink of facing similar challenges.

The author had always harbored a dream of entering government service, a vision that took root in his childhood. Growing up, he admired public servants and their impact on society, which inspired him to pursue a career dedicated to the greater good. However, as he transitioned into the corporate world, he encountered a stark contrast between his aspirations and the realities of corporate life. In his corporate job, the author experienced a lifestyle that was fast-paced and often driven by profit margins rather than people. He observed colleagues grappling with stress, long hours, and a relentless pursuit of targets that often overshadowed personal fulfillment. This environment gradually began to wear on him, leading to feelings of frustration and disillusionment.

As he navigated the corporate landscape, the author found himself reflecting on his childhood dreams. He began to question whether the sacrifices he was making for his job were worth it. The corporate culture, which prioritized competition and individual achievement, clashed with his values of service and community. Each day, he felt a growing sense of disconnect between his work and his aspirations.

Several pivotal moments further fueled his desire for change. He witnessed the toll that corporate pressures took on his colleagues' mental health, and he became increasingly aware of the societal challenges that public servants worked tirelessly to address. The realization that he could contribute positively to society reignited his passion for public service.

Ultimately, these experiences culminated in a decision to resign from his corporate position. The author embraced the uncertainty of leaving a stable job to pursue his dream of government service. This transition was not just a career shift; it was a profound change in lifestyle and values. He sought to align his daily work with his core beliefs, envisioning a future where he could make a meaningful impact on his community.

This narrative captures the author's journey of self-discovery, highlighting the stark contrasts between corporate life and the fulfilling path of public service. It illustrates the internal struggles and revelations that led him to reclaim his dreams, ultimately pursuing a career that resonated with his true calling. Through this transition, he found renewed purpose and the opportunity to contribute to a cause larger than himself

So, let's dive in and explore how he tackles this critical period and works towards achieving his goals.

About The Author

Writing a book has long been a cherished dream of mine. Initially, my intent was not to monetize this work but simply to have a book bearing my name. However, the practicalities of publishing necessitated placing a minimal price on it. Despite this, the process of writing has been incredibly fulfilling. When I embarked on this journey, I had no clear understanding of how to publish the book, nor was I certain it would ever be published. Yet, my unwavering belief in myself propelled me forward.

The primary purpose of this book is to offer motivation and guidance to those in their final year who remain unplaced and are grappling with frustration. While it is unrealistic to expect that frustration can be entirely avoided, my objective is to illuminate a pathway through these challenging times and to offer practical advice on overcoming obstacles. No matter how exceptional a student's abilities may be, they will inevitably face moments of intense frustration. The key lies in persistence and relentless practice. Even if you find yourself scoring poorly in aptitude tests or watching your peers excel in group discussions, maintaining composure and continuing to practice is crucial.

Consider the example of a close friend of mine who, despite consistently achieving average scores, achieved an astonishing first rank in an aptitude test on a renowned platform, Testpot.com. His performance left everyone, including myself, astounded. Naturally, I was concerned about my own standing, fearing that his exceptional results might overshadow my efforts. However, I chose to remain focused on my own preparation. It was later revealed that my friend had manipulated the test results by exploiting a loophole on the website, which allowed users to correct their answers after completion. This incident underscored a vital lesson: do not place undue faith in others' apparent successes. Instead, trust in your own abilities and efforts. Ultimately, the only person who can guide you through the various stages of your journey is only yourself.

Abhishek Kumar Singh

PART-1

CHAPTER ONE

The Pre-Final Year Journey

As pre-final year engineering students, we found ourselves deeply engrossed in observing the final year students who had gone through the rigorous process of preparing for interviews and aptitude exams. This observation was not just a matter of idle curiosity but a vital learning experience that offered us a glimpse into the complexities and challenges that awaited us. Our seniors often emphasized that while the exams themselves were not exceptionally difficult, the real challenge lay in achieving precision and managing the limited time effectively. These insights were invaluable, yet despite their efforts, the placement results often told a different story.

The stark reality was that very few names appeared on the placement notice boards after the results were declared. This was not necessarily because our seniors lacked the capability or skills to solve the questions but because of the disproportionate number of vacancies compared to the number of applicants. The intense competition meant that many missed out on opportunities due to minor shortfalls in their scores. Furthermore, companies employed a variety of additional criteria beyond just test scores—such as academic records, the presence of any gaps in education, or whether candidates had undergone improvement exams—which further narrowed down the pool of successful candidates. In some cases, rejection did not occur in the initial rounds but came as a shock during the final stages of selection, where companies scrutinized candidates' academic backgrounds alongside their interview performances.

These experiences were disheartening and, at times, demotivating. Watching the ups and downs faced by our seniors during the 5th and 6th semesters became a learning experience fraught with emotional challenges. The frustration often outweighed the motivation, making it difficult to stay focused and positive about our own prospects.

By the 6th semester, the process of preparing for aptitude exams had begun to take its toll on us. We found ourselves increasingly irritated and disillusioned with the preparation process, leading many of us to abandon our efforts prematurely. It was at this critical juncture that our Training and Placement Officer (TPO) shared a link with us. This link directed us to a practice test on a website, likely Naukri.com, just as we were transitioning into our 7th semester. This period marked a crucial turning point, as our seniors were nearing graduation and we were on the brink of our final year.

The year 2018 brought with it an atmosphere of trepidation. The placement statistics for that year painted a bleak picture, with no students from our Mechanical Engineering department having secured positions by April 2018. This lack of success fueled anxiety and fears that we would face similar challenges. However, a glimmer of hope emerged when one of our seniors, Subhra Mahapatra from NIT Manipur, managed to secure a position at Fluor Daniels, an esteemed Indian multinational corporation. This success story was soon followed by the placement of four more seniors in Denso Gurgaon, another reputable Indian MNC. These achievements provided a much-needed boost to our morale and instilled a sense of hope as we prepared for our final year.

The practice test shared by our TPO revealed a sobering reality. Many of us struggled with the test and abandoned it midway, highlighting significant gaps in our preparation. This experience exacerbated our anxieties about our performance in actual aptitude exams. The looming question of whether we would be able to secure placements added to our stress levels. As the end of the 6th semester approached, our focus shifted to preparing for our final exams, and we headed home for the summer vacation, albeit with a sense of uncertainty and urgency.

During the initial days of the vacation, I indulged in the comforts of home—enjoying familiar meals and spending quality time with family. As I prepared to enter my final year, relatives frequently inquired about the completion of my engineering degree. Their questions often carried an undertone of skepticism, as many believed that completing an engineering degree within the prescribed timeframe was unlikely. This skepticism was based on the experiences of others who had struggled to complete their degrees on time. Additionally, the perception that engineering was a less favorable career option, due to the experiences of those who had failed to secure jobs, further contributed to this negativity.

Reflecting on my decision to pursue engineering, the initial excitement of joining a prestigious institution gradually gave way to a realization of the challenges that lay ahead. The prospect of preparing for exams like GATE, once considered a viable option, did not initially captivate my interest. My focus was primarily on achieving a good CGPA, with the belief that companies would eventually visit our campus for recruitment. I had developed a habit of studying only a day or two before exams, which allowed me to secure decent grades but left me questioning whether this approach was sufficient to make me a competitive candidate.

As I entered my third year, I confronted a stark realization: despite being in my third year, I lacked a deep understanding of engineering concepts. My inability to answer common interview questions highlighted a significant knowledge gap, which contributed to my anxiety about how I would justify my high GPA despite my limited knowledge. This anxiety was compounded by sleepless nights filled with worry and self-doubt. It is often overlooked that behind the visible success of those who secure positions in multinational corporations lies immense effort and struggle, which is not immediately apparent to others.

A pivotal moment came when a friend of mine, who had invested in a GATE postal package course, expressed his determination to pursue a career in public sector undertakings or government organizations, rather than private firms. His commitment and focus contrasted sharply with my own lack of direction and ignited a sense of urgency in me. Despite my initial disappointment with a GATE preparation course that did not meet my expectations, I continued to observe my friend's diligent efforts. His resolve and dedication served as a stark reminder of what was required to achieve our goals.

As time progressed, I realized that my plans and dreams were moving slower than anticipated. The distractions of college life made it challenging to focus on GATE preparation. Watching my friends make significant strides while I struggled with indecision added to my frustration. I had to confront the possibility that securing a government job immediately after college might be unrealistic. Consequently, I decided to shift my focus to preparing for multinational corporations as a backup plan, acknowledging that serious GATE preparation might be impractical given the demands of college life.

Throughout this period of turmoil, I grappled with self-doubt and the pressure to meet societal expectations. Friends and relatives who disparaged private jobs while pursuing their own government job dreams further exacerbated my distress. Balancing self-doubt with the desire to enjoy college life proved challenging. Despite these struggles, I prioritized my happiness, recognizing that everything unfolds according to a higher plan. This journey, as described in this book, aims to offer insight and reassurance to those navigating similar challenges. As you reach the conclusion of 'Part II' of this book, I hope you gain a sense of understanding and patience, knowing that success comes in its own time.

Reflecting on the broader context of engineering education, it is evident that the journey from being a student to securing a desirable position is fraught with complexities. The competitive nature of the job market and the varied criteria employed by companies for selection mean that many students face significant challenges. The emotional and psychological impact of these challenges cannot be understated. The sense of inadequacy and frustration experienced by students, coupled with the societal pressures and expectations, creates a high-pressure environment that can be difficult to navigate.

The transition from academic life to the professional world is a critical phase that requires careful planning and preparation. The realization that a high CGPA alone may not be sufficient to secure a desirable job highlights the need for a more comprehensive approach to career development. This includes not only academic excellence but also practical skills, effective time management, and the ability to adapt to changing circumstances.

As students, it is essential to recognize that the journey towards securing a job is not a linear path. There will be setbacks and challenges along the way, and it is crucial to maintain resilience and determination. The experiences and insights shared in this book serve as a testament to the realities of this journey and offer valuable lessons for those embarking on a similar path.

In conclusion, the journey through engineering education and career preparation is a complex and multifaceted experience. The challenges faced by students, from academic pressures to societal expectations, are significant and require a nuanced understanding. By sharing these experiences and insights, this book aims to provide guidance and support to those navigating this challenging landscape. As you continue to explore the remaining sections of this book, I hope you find the inspiration and encouragement needed to persevere and succeed in your own journey.

Summary of this chapter:

The passage explores the experiences and challenges faced by engineering students, particularly in their final year, as they prepare for job placements and career opportunities. The narrative begins by reflecting on the observations of final-year students and their preparation strategies for interviews and aptitude exams. It notes that while the exams themselves were not inherently difficult, success required high accuracy and efficient time management. Despite this, many students found their names rarely appearing on the notice board after results were declared. This was often due to limited job vacancies and additional selection criteria set by companies, such as academic records and personal background factors. Some students were rejected not just in initial rounds but also in final stages due to these criteria.

The author describes their own experiences, starting from the 6th semester, when preparation for aptitude exams began but was quickly abandoned due to frustration. During this period, placement statistics for the Mechanical Engineering department were bleak, causing significant anxiety among students. A turning point occurred when a senior from the Mechanical department was placed in a notable Indian MNC, which boosted morale. This was followed by further placements, which provided a glimmer of hope.

The author recounts receiving a link to a practice aptitude test from their TPO (Training and Placement Officer) and the disheartening experience of struggling with the test. This frustration was compounded by the intense pressure and academic workload of the 6th semester, which eventually led to a focus on exams and summer vacation plans. The author reflects on the perceptions of family members regarding the completion of engineering studies, highlighting a general skepticism about the success of engineering graduates in the village.

As the author entered the 4th year, they realized the need for a strategic approach to career preparation. Despite initial indifference towards the GATE exam, the author recognized its importance as a potential pathway to government jobs and felt the need to seriously prepare. However, the challenge was compounded by distractions and lack of seriousness in the college environment. Friends who were dedicated to GATE preparation intensified the author's awareness of their own lack of progress, leading to feelings of inadequacy and guilt.

The author's journey through these academic and preparatory challenges is marked by a series of realizations about the inadequacies in their approach and the necessity of adopting a more disciplined strategy. They describe the emotional toll of seeing peers work hard while feeling unable to match their efforts. The narrative concludes with a message of hope and patience, emphasizing that despite the difficulties and setbacks, success and career achievements will come with time and persistent effort.

Message from the chapter:

The detailed passage conveys several key messages:

Comprehensive Preparation: Success in engineering and job placements requires more than just academic knowledge. It involves thorough preparation, accuracy in aptitude tests, and efficient time management. Students should not rely solely on high grades but also need to prepare strategically for exams and interviews.

Resilience Amidst Challenges: The journey to securing a job can be fraught with challenges and frustrations. It is crucial to remain resilient and adaptable despite setbacks, such as poor placement statistics or initial failures in tests.

Self-Belief and Perseverance: Maintaining self-belief and perseverance is essential. The narrative emphasizes the importance of believing in oneself and continuing to work hard even when progress seems slow or when faced with discouragement from external sources.

Strategic Planning: Effective career planning involves understanding and addressing one's weaknesses, setting clear goals, and adopting a disciplined approach to preparation. This includes managing distractions and making the most of available resources and opportunities.

Patience and Timing: Success does not come immediately. The passage highlights the need for patience and understanding that career achievements and opportunities will materialize with time and consistent effort.

In essence, the message is one of encouragement and practical advice for students navigating their final year and career preparation. It underscores the importance of perseverance, strategic planning, and self-belief in overcoming obstacles and achieving long-term career goals.

CHAPTER TWO

Seventh Semester

The end of vacation marked a significant transition for us as we returned to college, not just to continue our studies, but to confront a crucial phase in our academic journey: the appointment of Training and Placement Coordinators for our batch. The roles of these coordinators were pivotal—they were responsible for managing the Training & Placement (T&P) cell, handling communication with various companies, and ensuring that our profiles were forwarded to the appropriate Human Resources (HR) departments. This process was vital in facilitating our entry into the professional world.

Preparation for Placement Drives

The atmosphere was charged with a new sense of purpose. We were all acutely aware that our upcoming placements were not just about securing a job but about setting the stage for our future careers. As the coordinators took their positions, everyone began to work diligently. Profiles for the T&P Cell were created and optimized across various social media platforms to enhance communication with HR professionals. This digital presence was designed to streamline interactions and ensure that our profiles reached the right people.

We quickly moved from organizing our profiles to preparing ourselves for the actual placement drives. Lists of companies that would be conducting recruitment drives at different locations started circulating. Each company had its own set of requirements and processes, and the anticipation of these drives brought both excitement and anxiety.

Intensive Aptitude Preparation

With the drives on the horizon, our focus shifted to intensive preparation for aptitude tests. The atmosphere was one of frantic activity as we immersed ourselves in solving aptitude questions. Some of us opted for traditional resources like R.S. Aggarwal's books, renowned for their comprehensive coverage of aptitude questions. Others turned to various online platforms, which offered practice tests and question banks tailored to the demands of placement exams.

To provide some clarity on aptitude tests for those unfamiliar with them: Aptitude tests primarily assess your proficiency in basic mathematics, which typically covers concepts learned up to the 10th grade. These tests also incorporate reasoning skills and basic grammar. In essence, the syllabus for aptitude tests is built upon foundational mathematics and logical reasoning, supplemented by a grasp of language basics.

The Disconnect Between Engineering and Aptitude

One might wonder why, given the extensive focus on engineering subjects throughout our college years, so much emphasis was now placed on aptitude tests. The answer is straightforward yet disheartening. While engineering coursework is crucial for technical knowledge, placement success often hinges on excelling in aptitude exams. These tests serve as a preliminary filter, ensuring that only those who meet a certain standard progress to the next stages of the recruitment process.

This realization can be frustrating. Many of us had been led to believe that the primary criterion for campus placements was the interview process. However, the reality is more complex. Many companies conduct multiple rounds of testing before reaching the interview stage. These rounds might include written tests, group discussions, and other assessments. The interviews themselves can be multi-faceted, often comprising technical evaluations, HR rounds, coding tests (especially for IT and Computer Science students), and sometimes even presentation rounds.

The Intense Screening Process

The rigorous selection process is designed to identify the most capable candidates, often referred to as the "creamy layer." This extensive evaluation is not merely a formality but a strategy to ensure that companies attract and retain the best talent. For students like me, who struggled with communication skills and were inherently introverted, the prospect of navigating these rounds seemed daunting. The added pressure of competing against peers who seemed more polished and prepared only compounded our anxiety.

The Perception of Placement and Career Prospects

As an introvert with limited confidence in my soft skills, the prospect of securing a placement seemed almost unattainable. It was easy to succumb to the belief that my chances were slim, especially when faced with the intimidating array of tests and rounds. However, it's important to recognize that securing a job in India, despite the competitive environment, is indeed feasible. The process might be demanding, but it is not insurmountable. Many students find success through persistent effort and strategic preparation.

In summary, the period leading up to placement drives was marked by a blend of hope and apprehension. We engaged in rigorous preparation, navigating the complexities of aptitude tests, and adapting to the demands of the recruitment process. The reality of the multi-stage selection process became clear, underscoring the need for both technical proficiency and soft skills. Despite the challenges, it was essential to maintain perseverance and optimism, recognizing that opportunities could be within reach with the right preparation and mindset.

Summary

The passage explores the intense period of preparation and the recruitment process faced by college students gearing up for job placements. Upon returning from vacations, students are introduced to their new roles as Training and Placement (T&P) Coordinators, responsible for managing the placement process.

Their duties include handling the T&P cell, communicating with companies, and preparing profiles on social media platforms to enhance engagement with HR representatives.

As the placement drives approach, students dedicate themselves to solving aptitude questions, using resources such as R.S. Aggarwal books and various online platforms. Aptitude tests typically cover basic mathematics, reasoning, and grammar, derived from early education, which are crucial for passing initial screening rounds. Despite spending four years focusing on their engineering curriculum, students must excel in these aptitude tests to advance in the placement process.

The passage highlights a common misconception: that success in placements depends solely on the final interview. In reality, companies often use multiple rounds of assessments, including technical, HR, coding, and other specialized rounds, to select top candidates. For many students, especially those who struggle with communication and soft skills, this multi-round process can be daunting.

The passage reflects the reality that while securing a job through campus placements can be challenging, it is not insurmountable. The narrative underscores the need for students to be well-prepared and adaptable to the diverse requirements of the placement process.

Message

The passage conveys several key messages about the placement process and student preparation:

1. **Holistic Preparation is Crucial:** Success in campus placements requires more than academic knowledge. Students must also excel in aptitude tests, which cover fundamental skills like mathematics, reasoning, and grammar. This holistic approach to preparation involves not only understanding technical subjects but also mastering the skills needed for various rounds of assessments.

2. **Understanding the Recruitment Process:** The placement process often involves multiple stages beyond the final interview, such as technical assessments, coding tests, and HR interviews. Recognizing and preparing for these stages is essential for securing a job. The passage emphasizes that the placement process is rigorous and multi-faceted, with each stage designed to filter and identify the most qualified candidates.

3. **Addressing Skills Beyond Academics:** The passage highlights the challenge faced by students with weaker communication and soft skills. For such students, the placement process can seem particularly challenging. It is important for students to work on improving these skills alongside their technical knowledge to enhance their chances of success.

4. **Optimism and Perseverance:** Despite the difficulties and the intense competition, the passage reassures students that obtaining a job is achievable with dedication and strategic preparation. It encourages a positive mindset and emphasizes that overcoming these challenges is part of the journey to securing a successful placement.

5. **Adaptability and Strategic Preparation:** Students need to be adaptable and strategic in their preparation. This involves understanding the demands of each stage of the placement process and preparing accordingly. Strategic preparation can make a significant difference in navigating the complex recruitment landscape.

In summary, the passage serves as both a realistic portrayal of the placement process and a motivational guide, encouraging students to prepare thoroughly, develop essential skills, and remain optimistic in the face of challenges.

CHAPTER THREE

First Test

The vacation period had come to an end, and students returned to their college, now faced with the significant task of preparing for upcoming recruitment drives. A critical aspect of this preparation involved selecting and training the new batch of Training and Placement (T&P) Coordinators. Their responsibilities were crucial, encompassing the management of the T&P cell, preparation of databases, and communication with companies. This involved creating and maintaining profiles on various social media platforms to facilitate effective interaction with HR representatives and ensure smooth operations throughout the placement season.

As the placement drives approached, the first company scheduled to conduct its aptitude test at the college was Capgemini, a prominent multinational corporation. The test was administered in partnership with Cocubes.com, a platform known for its aptitude assessments. The test pattern was designed to be straightforward and manageable, reflecting the standard of practice tests available on Cocubes.com. Students preparing for this test could benefit from these practice tests, which mirrored the actual test's difficulty level.

The aptitude test, conducted on a specified date, was pivotal for students aiming to secure a position with Capgemini. The test included not only quantitative questions but also a paragraph writing section where candidates were required to compose a coherent response on a given topic within 200 words. This format was designed to evaluate not just mathematical and logical skills but also written communication abilities.

Since the test was held on campus, nearly all students participated. The results were announced promptly, revealing that around ten students had progressed to the next stage—the coding round. Given Capgemini's focus on IT roles, this round was anticipated and involved coding challenges. This stage proved particularly challenging for students from non-IT backgrounds, such as those in the Mechanical Engineering stream. These students were more accustomed to solving problems related to IC engines, Strength of Materials, and mechanical calculations rather than coding tasks. Consequently, only a few students from the Mechanical stream managed to solve the coding questions successfully, which highlighted the disparity between IT and non-IT students in this context.

By the end of the second round, only two students were selected for the final interview stage. These were candidates who had demonstrated exceptional skill and knowledge in the coding round. Observations from this process revealed that some students resorted to dishonest practices, such as obtaining answers from others. Such instances, while not uncommon, often lead to feelings of frustration and unfairness among the remaining candidates.

The passage reflects on the common perception that aptitude tests are deceptively simple, a notion that many students come to realize only through experience. The reality is that while the tests themselves might seem straightforward, success in placement drives requires rigorous practice and preparation. It's crucial to understand that while basic skills in aptitude and technical subjects are essential, the ability to handle the pressure of multiple assessment rounds and navigate various selection stages is equally important.

The passage offers several insights into the placement process and provides advice for students navigating this challenging period:

1. **Preparation and Practice:** The key to succeeding in aptitude tests and placement drives is extensive preparation and practice. This includes solving practice tests, understanding the test

pattern, and refining both technical and non-technical skills. Adequate preparation helps in building confidence and reducing stress during the actual test.

2. **Understanding Test Patterns:** Familiarizing oneself with the test pattern and types of questions is crucial. Practice tests and mock exams can provide a clear idea of what to expect, which helps in better preparation and reduces anxiety.

3. **Handling Multiple Rounds:** Many placement processes involve several rounds beyond the initial aptitude test, such as coding challenges, technical interviews, and HR interviews. Each round serves to assess different skill sets, and it is important to be prepared for all stages.

4. **Dealing with Frustration and Competition:** The placement season can be highly stressful, leading to frustrations and conflicts among students. It's important to manage stress effectively, stay focused on personal goals, and avoid getting involved in negative dynamics or office politics.

5. **Maintaining Humility and Confidence:** Success in initial rounds should be accompanied by humility. Students are advised to stay grounded and continue their preparation without becoming complacent. Confidence should be built on preparation and practice, rather than on mere luck or initial successes.

6. **Time Management and Prioritization:** Effective time management is essential during the placement season. Students should allocate time for both technical and non-technical preparation, including practice tests, mock interviews, and soft skills development.

7. **Resilience and Adaptability:** The ability to adapt to various test formats and requirements is crucial. Students should be resilient in the face of challenges and remain flexible in their approach to different types of assessments.

In conclusion, the passage underscores the importance of thorough preparation and a strategic approach to handling placement drives. It emphasizes that while the process may seem daunting, with the right preparation, mindset, and resilience, students can navigate these challenges effectively and enhance their chances of success.

Summary

The passage describes the experiences and challenges faced by students during their campus placement process. After the vacation period, students returned to college to find that it was time to select new Training and Placement (T&P) Coordinators, whose roles included managing the T&P cell and facilitating communication between students and prospective employers. These coordinators were responsible for preparing and sending students' profiles to companies and colleges for recruitment purposes.

The first major event was an aptitude test organized by Capgemini, a multinational corporation, in collaboration with Cocubes.com. The test was conducted at the college, and Cocubes.com set the level of difficulty to be relatively straightforward, with sample questions available for practice. The test included quantitative aptitude, logical reasoning, basic grammar, and a paragraph writing task.

Almost all students participated in the test, and around ten were selected for the next stage—the coding round. This round, essential for IT roles, proved challenging for non-IT students, especially those from Mechanical Engineering backgrounds. The disparity in preparation levels became evident, with only a few Mechanical Engineering students successfully solving the coding problems.

The results of the second round revealed that only two students advanced to the final interview stage. These students demonstrated strong coding skills, but the passage also noted some unethical practices, such as students seeking help during the test. This led to frustration among those who followed ethical practices.

The passage emphasizes the importance of preparation, noting that while aptitude tests might appear simple, thorough preparation and practice are essential. The placement process is marked by intense competition and stress, leading to interpersonal conflicts and office politics among peers. Students who do not succeed in early rounds may experience resentment and frustration, leading to conflicts within groups.

To navigate these challenges, students are advised to manage stress effectively, focus on preparation, and maintain a positive mindset. Engaging in practice tests and mock exams can help build confidence and improve performance. Humility and a balanced perspective are crucial, as is the ability to manage time effectively and adapt to different test formats and assessment criteria.

Message

The passage conveys several key messages about the campus placement process and the qualities needed to navigate it successfully:

1. **Importance of Thorough Preparation**: Success in campus placements requires more than just attending tests; it demands thorough preparation. This includes practicing aptitude questions, coding problems, and other relevant skills well in advance. Students should not rely solely on last-minute preparation but should build a solid foundation through consistent practice.

2. **Dealing with Stress and Frustration**: The placement process can be highly stressful and competitive. It is common for students to experience frustration and interpersonal conflicts during this period. Managing stress, maintaining a positive mindset, and focusing on personal goals can help students navigate these challenges effectively.

3. **Ethical Conduct**: Ethical behavior during the placement process is crucial. While some students may resort to seeking help or using unfair practices, maintaining integrity and following ethical practices is important for personal growth and long-term success.

4. **Humility and Balance**: Achieving success in the placement process should not lead to arrogance or complacency. It is

important for students to stay humble, recognize that success is the result of hard work and preparation, and continue striving for improvement.

5. **Time Management and Adaptability**: Effective time management and adaptability are essential skills. Students must balance preparation for technical assessments with other responsibilities and be prepared to handle various test formats and assessment criteria. Flexibility and resilience in the face of challenges are crucial for success.

6. **Personal Growth**: The placement process is not just about securing a job but also about personal development. It provides opportunities for students to develop resilience, problem-solving skills, and the ability to handle competitive pressures.

In summary, the passage underscores the need for comprehensive preparation, effective stress management, ethical conduct, humility, time management, and adaptability in navigating the campus placement process. It highlights that while the journey can be challenging, these qualities are essential for achieving success and personal growth.

CHAPTER FOUR

One More Pool Drive

The transition from academic life to professional employment is a crucial period for final-year college students. The period, often referred to as the placement season, brings with it a blend of excitement, anxiety, and intense preparation. For many students, including myself, this phase is not just about finding a job but also about overcoming personal and academic challenges. Here, I recount a detailed account of my journey through the placement process, highlighting the obstacles faced, unexpected turns, and ultimate lessons learned.

The Rigorous Placement Criteria

As the academic year resumed, the focus shifted from textbooks to preparing for job placements. The placement process involved a series of tests, interviews, and eliminations, which were designed by various companies to filter out the most suitable candidates. These companies often set stringent criteria that candidates had to meet in order to participate in their selection processes.

One of the companies that came to our college was particularly stringent with its criteria. This company, known for its prestigious reputation, set a policy that excluded any student with a gap year—either after completing their 12th grade or during their B.Tech— from participating in their selection process. This criterion was a significant hurdle for many students, including myself, as I had taken a gap year after my 12th grade. Despite my strong academic record and fervent desire to work with this company, the policy meant that I was initially disqualified from the selection process.

The Disheartening Exclusion

The strict adherence to these criteria by the placement coordinators meant that once the list of eligible candidates was finalized, there was little room for exceptions. Despite my repeated requests and hopes that my academic performance might sway the decision, the HR representatives from the company remained firm on their policy. My name was consequently removed from the list of candidates allowed to participate in the placement drive.

This exclusion was a severe blow to my aspirations. I had invested considerable time and effort into preparing for this drive, and the sudden disqualification was both unexpected and disheartening. I had to come to terms with the reality that my dream of working with this company might not materialize.

An Unexpected Turn of Events

Just as I was beginning to accept this setback, an unexpected turn of events occurred. The night before the placement drive at NIT Silchar, when everyone was preparing for the journey, I received surprising news. My branch coordinator, who had previously expressed helplessness regarding my situation, approached me with a new list of participants. To my astonishment, my name was on this list.

The news was met with mixed emotions. While my coordinator was visibly thrilled, my own feelings were a blend of surprise and anxiety. I had not anticipated being included in the drive, and with the placement process fast approaching, I was unprepared for the upcoming challenge.

The Challenge of Last-Minute Preparation

It was around 1:30 A.M. when my branch coordinator informed me of my inclusion in the list. As I had been preparing for another placement drive scheduled shortly after, I had not adequately prepared for the L&T Heavy's drive. This sudden inclusion meant that I had to scramble to get ready. I had to wake up at 4:00 A.M. for the journey to NIT Silchar, and my preparation was lacking.

With limited time to prepare, I focused on organizing my formal attire and gathering essential items for the journey. The realization that I was underprepared added to my stress. I had to balance preparations for the drive at NIT Silchar with the upcoming placement drive at NIT Nagaland. The challenge of managing both drives simultaneously was overwhelming.

The Journey to NIT Silchar

The journey to NIT Silchar was both physically and mentally taxing. We traveled by a Winger, a type of road vehicle, which took us through the hilly terrain of Manipur. The winding roads and sharp turns made the journey uncomfortable, and many of us struggled with motion sickness. The long and arduous journey only added to the stress of the placement process.

Despite the discomfort, we pressed on, driven by the hope of making a good impression at the drive. The night before, I had revised my notes on technical subjects, but my preparation was far from thorough. As the journey progressed, I tried to mentally prepare myself for the placement tests and interviews ahead.

The Placement Drive Experience

Upon arriving at NIT Silchar, we participated in the pre-placement talk, which provided an overview of the company and the selection process. The placement drive included a written test, which was more challenging than I had anticipated. The test featured a sectional cut-off for each section, adding to the complexity of the assessment.

The test lasted for an hour and assessed various skills, including technical knowledge and problem-solving abilities. After completing the test, we had a brief break and enjoyed some snacks. The uncertainty of the outcome lingered as we awaited the results. Despite my best efforts, the results were disappointing, and I did not advance past this stage.

Facing Additional Challenges

Adding to the difficulty, I had another placement drive scheduled at NIT Nagaland shortly after the L&T Heavy's drive. The process of preparing for and attending multiple drives in quick succession was exhausting. Unfortunately, I faced rejection at the NIT Nagaland drive as well.

The repeated rejections were demoralizing, especially given my introverted nature and perceived lack of confidence. Many peers and relatives had doubted my ability to succeed in interviews, questioning how I could overcome these challenges given my communication skills. However, I remained determined and continued to prepare diligently.

The Power of Persistence and Preparation

The key lesson from this experience was the importance of persistence. Despite facing multiple rejections, I remained focused on my goal and continued to prepare. I realized that success in the placement process was not solely about initial impressions but also about persistence and thorough preparation.

The ability to answer questions accurately, even with less-than-perfect communication skills, was crucial. The placement process is not always about immediate success but about perseverance and continuous effort. Even when faced with setbacks, it is essential to stay focused and keep working towards your goals.

The Final Outcome

Despite the challenges and rejections, my persistence eventually paid off. Through continuous preparation and determination, I secured a job offer. The journey through the placement season was a test of resilience, adaptability, and dedication. It taught me valuable lessons about handling rejection, preparing thoroughly, and staying positive in the face of adversity.

Conclusion

The placement season is a defining and challenging phase in a student's academic journey. It involves navigating stringent criteria, facing setbacks, and preparing for various assessments. The experience of overcoming obstacles and persistent efforts contributes significantly to personal and professional growth. The placement process highlights that success is not always immediate but often requires perseverance, thorough preparation, and a positive mindset. Ultimately, the journey through placements is a valuable learning experience that prepares students for future success in their careers.

Summary

Introduction to Placement Challenges

The passage recounts the journey of a final-year student navigating the challenging process of college placements. It provides a detailed narrative of the various obstacles faced during the placement season, emphasizing the rigorous selection criteria set by companies, the personal struggles experienced, and the eventual lessons learned.

Stringent Company Criteria

The placement process involved various companies, each with its own set of criteria for selection. One prominent company, known for its prestigious reputation, had a strict policy that excluded students who had taken a gap year, whether after their 12th grade or during their B.Tech. This policy created significant hurdles for many students, including the narrator, who had a gap year after their 12th grade. Despite their strong academic performance and eagerness to join the company, they were initially disqualified from the selection process due to this criterion.

The Unexpected Inclusion

Despite the initial disqualification, the narrator experienced an unexpected turn of events. On the night before the placement drive at NIT Silchar, they were surprised to find their name on the final list of participants. This sudden inclusion came as a shock, especially given their lack of preparation. The narrator was initially overwhelmed, as they had not anticipated being part of the drive and were unprepared both mentally and logistically.

The Journey to NIT Silchar

The journey to NIT Silchar was fraught with difficulties. The students traveled by a Winger through hilly terrain, which was physically uncomfortable and led to motion sickness for many. Despite the challenging conditions, the narrator and their peers remained hopeful about the placement drive.

The Placement Drive Experience

At NIT Silchar, the narrator participated in the pre-placement talk and the written test. The test was challenging, with a sectional cut-off for each section, adding to the difficulty. Despite their efforts, the narrator did not advance past this stage. The results were disappointing, and the subsequent placement drive at NIT Nagaland also resulted in rejection.

Personal Challenges and Rejections

The repeated rejections were disheartening, especially given the narrator's introverted nature and perceived lack of confidence. Their peers and relatives had doubts about their ability to succeed, particularly in interviews. Despite these challenges, the narrator remained determined and continued to prepare diligently.

Lessons Learned

The narrator's persistence eventually led to success. The experience highlighted the importance of perseverance, thorough preparation, and maintaining a positive mindset. The passage underscores that success in the placement process is not immediate but requires continuous effort and resilience. The narrator's journey through multiple rejections and challenges demonstrated that success is achieved through dedication and a willingness to keep trying, even in the face of adversity.

Message

The passage conveys several important messages:

1. **Rigorous Selection Criteria:** The placement process can be stringent, with companies often setting strict criteria that can disqualify many candidates. Students need to be aware of these criteria and understand that meeting them is crucial for advancing in the selection process.

2. **Unexpected Opportunities:** Even when faced with disqualification or setbacks, unexpected opportunities can arise. The narrator's inclusion in the placement drive at the last moment serves as a reminder that circumstances can change, and students should remain prepared for any eventuality.

3. **The Importance of Preparation:** Adequate preparation is essential for success in placement drives. The narrator's lack of preparation led to initial failures, emphasizing the need to be well-prepared for all aspects of the placement process, including tests and interviews.

4. **Resilience and Perseverance:** The journey through placement drives often involves facing rejection and challenges. The passage highlights the importance of resilience and perseverance in overcoming these obstacles. Success may not come immediately, but persistence and continued effort are key to achieving one's goals.

5. **Positive Mindset:** Maintaining a positive mindset, even in the face of setbacks, is crucial. The narrator's eventual success, despite initial rejections, demonstrates that a positive attitude and determination can lead to eventual success.

6. **Value of Continuous Effort:** Success in placement and career pursuits often requires ongoing effort and adaptability. The narrator's experience underscores that consistent effort and a willingness to adapt are essential for long-term success.

Overall, the passage serves as a comprehensive account of the placement process, illustrating the challenges, unexpected turns, and the ultimate importance of persistence and preparation in achieving career goals.

CHAPTER FIVE

After-Effects

Experiencing repeated setbacks, especially when they concern pivotal moments like job placements, can be an incredibly disheartening and frustrating experience. The journey of not being selected for the second time can feel like a blow to one's dreams and aspirations, making it a poignant moment to reflect on how to navigate future uncertainties.

At this juncture, a profound realization began to set in: the realization that L&T, a notable company that had previously visited our campus for recruitment, might not return for future placements. This thought stirred a sense of urgency, compelling me to reassess my strategy and consider alternative options. It became evident that relying solely on a single company's visit for career prospects was an untenable strategy. As a result, a comprehensive evaluation of other potential opportunities was necessary to ensure that I did not miss out on any viable prospects.

The process of re-evaluating one's career strategy was not undertaken in isolation. It was a collective effort among peers, who, despite their shared sense of uncertainty and disappointment, found solace in each other's company. Our shared experiences led to a sense of camaraderie, and to cope with the mounting stress, we engaged in light-hearted conversations. Our discussions often veered towards humorous anecdotes from our hostel life, serving as a much-needed diversion from the anxiety of the moment. This laughter was not merely an escape but a vital mechanism for managing stress and maintaining mental well-being.

However, the underlying concern remained: the limited number of companies visiting our campus created a narrow window of opportunity. This limitation became more pronounced when we observed that our college administration appeared disengaged from actively facilitating new recruitment avenues. The promises of hiring a new Training and Placement Officer (TPO) with relevant corporate experience remained unfulfilled. This inaction left us grappling with a feeling of helplessness and frustration. We were confronted with a harsh reality where the administrative support we had hoped for was absent, and we were left to navigate this challenging landscape on our own.

It is crucial to acknowledge that this narrative is shared not to dishearten or demotivate but to provide a realistic perspective on the challenges faced during job placements. By presenting these challenges candidly, I aim to offer a glimpse into the resilience required to overcome such obstacles. This narrative is intended to serve as a guide for others who may find themselves in similar situations, helping them to understand that perseverance and adaptability are key.

Communicating the news of rejection to one's parents adds another layer of complexity to the situation. The process of explaining rejection can be emotionally taxing, particularly when parents are unfamiliar with the nuances of the selection process. The difficulty lies in conveying the intricacies of the rejection, as well as managing the emotional responses of those who care about you. Parents, often with the best intentions, may focus on the number of rejections rather than understanding the broader context. This can inadvertently increase the pressure on the individual, exacerbating feelings of self-doubt and anxiety.

Despite these challenges, it is essential to approach the situation with a positive mindset. One effective strategy is to focus on the preparation for future opportunities rather than dwelling on past rejections. It is tempting to revisit and review basic concepts in response to a failed placement attempt. However, a more strategic approach involves understanding the specific requirements of the next company's recruitment process. Each company has its own set of criteria, question patterns, and difficulty levels, which can differ significantly from previous experiences.

To effectively prepare for future placement exams, one should thoroughly research the companies that will visit the campus. This involves studying the company's profile, understanding their recruitment trends, and reviewing previous placement papers. These papers are often available online and can provide valuable insights into the types of questions typically asked and the level of difficulty one can expect. By aligning preparation efforts with the specific requirements of each company, candidates can enhance their chances of success.

Additionally, adopting a proactive approach towards preparation can mitigate the impact of setbacks. Instead of simply brushing up on aptitude basics, it is more beneficial to tailor your preparation based on the trends and patterns observed in previous exams of the prospective company. Each company may emphasize different aspects of the aptitude test, and being aware of these nuances can significantly improve performance.

In conclusion, navigating the challenges of job placements requires a blend of resilience, adaptability, and strategic preparation. The experiences shared here highlight the importance of managing stress, seeking support, and focusing on targeted preparation to overcome setbacks. By adopting a thoughtful approach and learning from each experience, individuals can better equip themselves to face future challenges and ultimately achieve their career goals.

Summary

The passage recounts the personal experience of facing rejection in job placements after not being selected for a second time by the company L&T. This repeated failure led to a realization that the company might not return for future recruitment, highlighting a critical need to explore alternative opportunities.

1. Initial Reactions and Emotional Impact:

- The immediate reaction to the rejection was a sense of shattered dreams and realization of limited opportunities. The narrator, along with peers, was initially consumed by disappointment, as L&T was one of the few major companies that visited their campus.

2. Coping Mechanisms:

- To manage the stress of the situation, the narrator and peers engaged in discussions about humorous hostel anecdotes. This provided emotional relief and a way to cope with the anxiety surrounding the result declaration.

3. Administrative Challenges:

- The passage highlights a lack of effective administrative support from the college. The college had made promises to hire a new Training and Placement Officer (TPO) with corporate experience, but these promises were not fulfilled, leaving students feeling helpless and unsupported.

4. Emotional Strain of Informing Parents:

- Informing parents about the rejection was particularly challenging. The narrator describes the difficulty in communicating the reasons for rejection and the added pressure of dealing with parental disappointment. The parents' focus on the number of rejections added to the stress of the situation.

5. Preparation Strategies:

- The passage advises against focusing solely on reviewing past aptitude test concepts. Instead, it emphasizes the importance of researching the companies that will visit the campus, understanding their specific recruitment trends, and preparing according to their unique requirements. This includes studying previous placement papers and adapting to the company's style of questioning.

6. Future Outlook:

- The narrative concludes with a perspective on how such setbacks, though challenging, can ultimately contribute to personal growth and resilience. The experience of navigating these difficulties can strengthen one's ability to handle future challenges and achieve career goals.

Message
1. Resilience in the Face of Setbacks:

- The passage underscores the importance of resilience when dealing with repeated rejections and setbacks. It emphasizes that setbacks are a common part of the job placement process and should be viewed as challenges to overcome rather than insurmountable obstacles.

2. Importance of Emotional and Social Support:

- Maintaining mental well-being is crucial during stressful times. Engaging in supportive interactions with peers and finding ways to alleviate stress, such as through humor, are essential for managing the emotional impact of rejections.

3. Proactive and Strategic Preparation:

- Effective preparation for future job placements involves more than just revisiting basic concepts. It requires understanding the specific requirements and trends of each prospective company. By tailoring preparation to the company's unique recruitment process, candidates can improve their chances of success.

****4. Navigating Administrative and Institutional Limitations:**

- The lack of administrative support from the college highlights a broader issue of institutional responsibility. Students may face situations where the support they need is not available, and they must adapt by taking proactive steps to find and create opportunities on their own.

****5. Managing Parental Expectations and Communication:**

- Communicating with parents about rejections involves addressing their concerns and managing their expectations. It's important to navigate these conversations with sensitivity and provide context to help them understand the broader picture.

****6. Long-Term Growth and Adaptability:**

- The passage suggests that experiencing and overcoming these difficulties can contribute to long-term personal and professional growth. Each setback offers a learning opportunity that can build resilience and prepare individuals for future challenges.

In essence, the detailed message of the passage is to encourage individuals to view setbacks as learning experiences, to seek and use emotional support effectively, to prepare strategically for future opportunities, and to communicate thoughtfully with those who are emotionally invested in their success. This approach not only helps in dealing with immediate challenges but also fosters personal growth and adaptability in the long term.

CHAPTER SIX

Selection Methods

Embarking on the journey of campus placements can be both exciting and daunting. The process typically involves several stages, including aptitude tests, technical assessments, and interviews. This guide aims to provide an in-depth understanding of each stage, offering practical advice, strategies, and personal insights to help you navigate the complexities of campus placements effectively.

6.1 Aptitude Test Preparation

The aptitude test is often the first hurdle in the campus placement process. It assesses your basic mathematical skills, analytical reasoning, and English proficiency. Here's how to prepare comprehensively for this test:

6.1.1 Understanding the Content

Mathematics: The aptitude test generally covers mathematical concepts up to the 10th-grade level. Key areas include:

- **Profit & Loss:** Understand concepts like cost price, selling price, profit, and loss percentage.
- **Percentages:** Focus on calculations involving percentage increase/decrease, percentage profit/loss, and percentage-based problems.
- **Averages:** Practice finding the mean, median, and mode of a set of numbers.
- **Alligation & Mixtures:** Learn how to solve problems related to mixing different quantities and concentrations.

- **Simple Interest (SI) & Compound Interest (CI):** Understand formulas and problems involving interest calculations.
- **Time and Work:** Solve problems related to work done by individuals or groups within a given time frame.
- **Number Systems:** Familiarize yourself with concepts like divisibility rules, factors, and multiples.
- **Mensuration:** Practice problems involving area, volume, and surface area of geometric shapes.
- **Permutation & Combinations:** Learn how to solve problems involving arrangements and selections.

Analytical Reasoning: This section tests your logical and reasoning abilities through:

- **Blood Relations:** Solve problems on family relationships and their logical connections.
- **Data Sufficiency:** Determine whether the provided data is enough to answer a question.
- **Data Interpretation:** Analyze and interpret data presented in tables, charts, and graphs.
- **Syllogisms:** Deduce logical conclusions from given statements.
- **Coding & Decoding:** Solve problems that involve deciphering coded messages.
- **Series Problems:** Identify patterns and solve sequence-based problems.
- **Analogy:** Solve problems that involve finding relationships between pairs of words or numbers.

English Proficiency: This section evaluates your command of the English language through:

- **Synonyms & Antonyms:** Identify words with similar or opposite meanings.
- **Comprehensive Paragraph-Based Questions:** Answer questions based on passages provided.

- **Active & Passive Voice:** Convert sentences between active and passive voice.
- **Direct & Indirect Speech:** Transform sentences from direct to indirect speech and vice versa.
- **Sentence Rearrangement:** Rearrange jumbled sentences into a coherent structure.
- **Sentence Jumbles:** Solve problems involving jumbled words or phrases.

6.1.2 Preparation Strategies

Practice Tests:

- **Simulated Tests:** Regularly take practice tests to simulate the actual exam environment. This helps in managing time and pressure during the real test. Websites like Indiabix.com and Testpot.com offer numerous practice tests and sample questions.

Study Materials:

- **Comprehensive Notes:** Obtain detailed study notes from reliable sources. These can be downloaded from educational websites or borrowed from peers who have attended coaching institutes. Comprehensive notes will cover all relevant topics and problem-solving techniques.

YouTube Resources:

- **Educational Channels:** Utilize free YouTube tutorials from channels such as Dinesh Miglani Tutorials and Wi-Fi Study. These channels provide valuable explanations and problem-solving strategies for various aptitude topics.

Mock Tests:

- **Organize Practice Sessions:** Request your Training and Placement Officer (TPO) to arrange regular Computer-Based Tests (CBTs) or mock tests. These sessions help you become familiar with the test format and gain practical experience.

6.2 Effective Preparation Techniques
6.2.1 Utilizing Online Resources
Free Practice Websites:

- **Diverse Platforms:** Explore various online platforms offering practice tests, quizzes, and sample questions. Regular practice on these platforms will enhance your problem-solving skills and familiarity with different question types.

Additional Study Resources:

- **Books and Guides:** In addition to online resources, use books and guides specifically designed for aptitude tests. These materials often include practice questions, solutions, and explanations to help you understand key concepts.

6.2.2 Reviewing Basics
Note-taking:

- **Detailed Summaries:** Create detailed notes summarizing key concepts and problem-solving techniques. Regularly review these notes to reinforce your understanding and ensure you can quickly recall important information during the test.

Daily Practice:

- **Consistent Study Routine:** Allocate specific time each day for solving practice problems and reviewing concepts. Consistent practice helps in maintaining familiarity with different question types and improving overall performance.

6.3 Understanding Test Administration and Platforms
6.3.1 Test Platforms
Company-specific Platforms:

- **Custom Testing Solutions:** Some companies develop their own testing platforms tailored to their specific requirements. Familiarize yourself with the format and features of these platforms if possible to ensure you are well-prepared.

Test Formats:

- **Online vs. Paper-Based Tests:** Understand the differences between online and paper-based tests. Online tests often feature interactive elements and time limits, while paper-based tests require manual calculations and answer marking.

6.3.2 Marking and Result Declaration
Sectional Performance:

- **Focused Evaluation:** Companies may assess candidates based on their performance in specific sections relevant to the job role. For example, a Data Analyst company might prioritize performance in Data Interpretation.

Overall Evaluation:

- **Holistic Assessment:** In addition to sectional scores, companies might consider your overall GPA and performance in areas aligned with the job profile. Tailor your preparation to excel in sections critical to the company's needs.

6.4 Interview Round Preparation
6.4.1 Preparing for Interviews
Company Research:

- **Interview Trends:** Research the company's interview patterns and common questions. Understanding the company's focus areas, such as case studies for Data Analyst roles or technical skills for IT positions, will help you prepare effectively.

Personal Experience:

- **Real-life Examples:** Share personal experiences of handling interviews and provide insights into common pitfalls. For instance, managing interview pressure effectively can significantly impact your performance.

6.4.2 Balancing Technical and Non-Technical Skills
Technical Proficiency:

- **Role-Specific Knowledge:** For technical roles, ensure you are well-versed in relevant technical knowledge. This includes understanding practical applications and problem-solving in your field. Review core technical concepts and practice related problems.

Soft Skills:

- **Communication and Problem-Solving:** Develop strong soft skills such as communication, problem-solving, and critical thinking. These skills are essential for handling situational questions and demonstrating your ability to fit within the company culture.

6.4.3 Handling Practical Questions and Pressure
Practical Approach:

- **Problem-Solving Skills:** During interviews, especially with experienced HR professionals, focus on solving practical problems rather than purely theoretical questions. For example, if asked about Bending Moment and Shear Force Diagrams, emphasize your ability to solve practical problems related to these concepts.

Stress Management:

- **Techniques for Calmness:** Learn techniques to manage interview pressure, such as deep breathing or relaxation exercises before the interview. Staying calm and focused during the interview will help you perform better.

6.4.4 Interview Techniques
Effective Communication:

- **Clear Explanation:** Clearly explain your problem-solving process and reasoning, even if you are unsure about the exact answer. Effective communication can demonstrate your logical thinking and problem-solving abilities.

Impressing HR Professionals:

- **Practical Application:** Experienced HR professionals may focus on your ability to apply knowledge practically rather than theoretical accuracy. Showcase your practical skills and common sense in problem-solving.

Conclusion

Preparing for campus interviews involves a structured and multifaceted approach. By thoroughly preparing for aptitude tests, utilizing online resources, practicing consistently, and understanding the specific requirements of each company, you can enhance your chances of success. Balancing technical knowledge with soft skills and managing interview pressure are key components of a successful placement strategy. Adapting to the unique needs of each company and demonstrating a practical approach will help you stand out in the competitive placement process.

Summary of Key Points:

1. **Aptitude Test Preparation:**

    ◦ Focus on mathematics, analytical reasoning, and English proficiency.
    ◦ Use practice tests, comprehensive study materials, and online resources.
    ◦ Regularly take mock tests to simulate real exam conditions.

2. **Effective Preparation Techniques:**

    ◦ Utilize free practice websites and additional study resources.
    ◦ Create detailed notes and practice consistently.

3. **Understanding Test Administration:**

    ◦ Familiarize yourself with company-specific test platforms and formats.
    ◦ Focus on sectional performance and overall evaluation criteria.

4. **Interview Round Preparation:**

    ◦ Research company interview trends and prepare accordingly.
    ◦ Balance technical knowledge with soft skills.
    ◦ Handle practical questions and interview pressure effectively.

By following this comprehensive guide, you can navigate the campus placement process with confidence and increase your chances of securing a desired position.

6.5 Now how do companies take tests?

When it comes to administering aptitude tests during campus placements, companies employ a variety of methods. Understanding these methods can help you better prepare for the tests and adapt to different scenarios. Here's a detailed overview of the approaches companies use and what you should know about each:

6.5.1. Company-Developed Test Platforms

6.5.1.1. Custom Platforms:

- **Description:** Some companies develop their own proprietary test platforms to conduct aptitude tests. These platforms are tailored to the company's specific requirements and may include unique features or question formats.
- **Features:** Custom platforms may offer various functionalities such as adaptive testing (where the difficulty of questions adjusts based on your performance), timed sections, and integrated technical assessments.
- **Preparation Tips:**

  - **Familiarize Yourself:** If you know in advance that a company uses a custom platform, try to gather information about its features and interface. Sometimes companies provide sample tests or tutorials to help candidates get accustomed to the platform.
  - **Practice on Similar Platforms:** Use practice tests from platforms with similar features to become comfortable with navigating online tests. Websites offering mock tests or educational platforms may provide insights into the kind of features you might encounter.

6.5.1.2. Integrated Tools:

- **Description:** Companies may also integrate their tests with tools for real-time monitoring, anti-cheating mechanisms, and instant feedback. These tools ensure the integrity of the testing process and provide immediate results.

- **Features:** Tools may include webcam monitoring, browser lockdowns, and proctoring features. They might also offer real-time scoring and detailed performance analytics.
- **Preparation Tips:**

  - **Understand the Environment:** Ensure you are familiar with the technical requirements of the test, such as browser compatibility and hardware specifications. Check if the company provides any guidelines or technical requirements for the test.

6.5.2. Collaboration with Aptitude Test Providers
6.5.2.1. Third-Party Platforms:

- **Description:** Many companies collaborate with established aptitude test providers or platforms that specialize in conducting standardized assessments. These platforms are designed to handle large volumes of test-takers and provide a uniform testing experience.
- **Features:** Third-party platforms often include a range of practice tests, question banks, and advanced analytics. They might also offer features such as timed tests, automatic scoring, and detailed performance reports.
- **Preparation Tips:**

  - **Utilize Practice Tests:** Make use of practice tests offered by these third-party platforms. Familiarize yourself with the question types and test formats that are commonly used. Websites such as Talview, HackerRank, or Codility (for coding tests) often provide sample questions and practice opportunities.
  - **Review Platform-Specific Guidelines:** Each third-party platform might have specific guidelines or instructions. Review these instructions carefully to avoid any technical

issues on the test day.

6.5.2.2. Paper-Based Tests:

- **Description:** Although less common in the digital age, some companies still administer paper-based aptitude tests. These tests are usually conducted in a controlled environment and involve traditional paper-and-pencil questions.
- **Features:** Paper-based tests might include multiple-choice questions, numerical problems, and logical reasoning questions. They often require manual calculations and answer recording.
- **Preparation Tips:**

  - **Practice Traditional Methods:** Since paper-based tests don't offer the convenience of digital tools, practice solving problems manually. Work on improving your calculation speed and accuracy.
  - **Get Comfortable with Physical Tests:** If you're used to digital tests, take the time to practice with physical question papers. This helps in getting accustomed to the format and time constraints of paper-based testing.

6.5.3. *Test Format Variations*
6.5.3.1. Online Tests:

- **Description:** Online tests are conducted via digital platforms and are increasingly popular due to their convenience and efficiency. They can be administered at home or in a designated testing center.
- **Features:** Online tests often include interactive elements, such as drag-and-drop questions or simulations. They may also include automatic time tracking and instant feedback.
- **Preparation Tips:**

- ◦ **Simulate Test Conditions:** Take online practice tests to get used to the digital environment. Ensure your internet connection is stable and that you are familiar with the test's interface and navigation.
- ◦ **Practice Time Management:** Online tests are often timed, so practice solving questions quickly and accurately to improve your time management skills.

6.5.3.2. Hybrid Tests:

- **Description:** Some companies use a hybrid approach, combining online and offline elements. For example, an initial online test might be followed by an in-person assessment or interview.
- **Features:** Hybrid tests can include a mix of digital and physical components, such as an online quiz followed by a hands-on technical assessment or problem-solving session.
- **Preparation Tips:**

  - ◦ **Prepare for Both Scenarios:** Be ready for both online and offline testing formats. Practice digital tests and also be prepared for any in-person components that might require physical problem-solving or technical skills.

Adapting to Different Test Scenarios
****1. Preparation for Custom Platforms:**

- **Research the Platform:** If you know a company uses a custom platform, research it in advance. Look for any available resources, tutorials, or sample tests provided by the company.
- **Technical Setup:** Ensure your computer and internet setup meet the platform's requirements. Conduct a technical check to avoid last-minute issues.

****2. Preparation for Third-Party Platforms:**

- **Use Platform Resources:** Take advantage of practice tests and resources provided by the third-party platform. Familiarize yourself with the types of questions and the interface used by the platform.
- **Follow Guidelines:** Adhere to any specific guidelines or instructions given by the platform to ensure a smooth testing experience.

****3. Preparation for Paper-Based Tests:**

- **Practice Manually:** Solve practice questions manually to improve your speed and accuracy. Get comfortable with traditional problem-solving methods.
- **Simulate Test Conditions:** Take timed practice tests on paper to mimic the test environment and build confidence.

Conclusion

Understanding how companies administer aptitude tests and preparing for different testing scenarios can significantly impact your performance during campus placements. By familiarizing yourself with the various test platforms and formats, you can approach the testing process with greater confidence and competence. Whether dealing with custom platforms, third-party providers, or paper-based tests, comprehensive preparation and adaptability are key to succeeding in the aptitude test phase of campus placements.

In summary:

- **Custom Platforms:** Research and prepare for unique features and functionalities.
- **Third-Party Platforms:** Utilize practice tests and follow platform-specific guidelines.
- **Paper-Based Tests:** Practice manual problem-solving and simulate test conditions.

By addressing each aspect of test administration, you'll be well-prepared to tackle any aptitude test challenge that comes your way during campus placements.

6.6 How Do Companies Mark and Declare Results?

The process of marking and declaring results in campus placement tests involves several nuanced criteria that can vary from one company to another. Understanding these criteria is crucial for tailoring your preparation and improving your chances of success. Here's a detailed look at how companies handle marking and result declaration:

6.6.1 Criteria for Marking

1. Sectional Performance:

- **Importance of Specific Sections:** Companies often emphasize performance in specific sections that align with the job role. For example, a Data Analyst position will likely prioritize your performance in the Data Interpretation section over other areas.
- **Scoring Systems:** Tests may have sectional cutoffs or weightages where certain sections are given more importance based on the job profile. For instance, if a company values analytical skills highly, the analytical reasoning section might carry more weight in the final score.

2. Overall Performance:

- **Aggregate Scores:** In addition to sectional scores, companies may consider your overall performance. A strong overall score, combined with good performance in critical sections, can enhance your chances of moving forward in the selection process.
- **Cutoff Scores:** Some companies set an overall cutoff score that candidates must meet to be considered for further stages. These cutoffs can be influenced by the number of available positions and the overall performance of the candidates.

3. GPA Consideration:

- **Academic Performance:** Companies sometimes take your Grade Point Average (GPA) into account, especially if they use it as a tiebreaker or additional criterion. A higher GPA can sometimes compensate for lower performance in certain sections, though this varies by company.

6.6.2 *How Results Are Declared*

1. Results Based on Sectional Performance:

- **Targeted Evaluation:** For job roles requiring specific skills, companies might focus on performance in sections most relevant to the role. For example, if you're applying for a Data Analyst role, exceptional performance in Data Interpretation and related sections is crucial.
- **Sectional Cutoffs:** Companies may set cutoffs for individual sections. If you do not meet these cutoffs, you may not proceed to the next stage, regardless of your overall score.

2. Results Based on Overall Scores:

- **Comprehensive Evaluation:** In some cases, companies look at the total score and compare it against other candidates. High performance across all sections, even if not top in every section, can be a positive factor.
- **Ranking and Selection:** Candidates are often ranked based on their total scores. Those with higher rankings are more likely to be selected for interviews or further assessments.

3. Role-Specific Focus:

- **Customized Results:** Companies tailor their evaluation process based on the nature of the job. For example, IT companies that include coding questions may weigh coding performance heavily. If you perform well in other sections but poorly in coding, it might affect your overall selection.

- **Job Alignment:** Align your preparation with the job role. If the role requires strong analytical skills, focus on improving your performance in relevant sections. Companies are more likely to select candidates who align well with their job requirements.

6.6.3 Personal Experience Insights
1. Analyzing My Experience:

- **Capgemini Example:** Reflecting on my experience, my rejection in Capgemini's test was due to weak coding skills, despite performing well in other areas. This underscores the importance of focusing on all relevant sections, especially those critical to the job role.
- **Learning from Feedback:** Use feedback from previous tests to identify areas for improvement. If specific sections are emphasized, allocate more time to strengthen those areas.

2. Strategic Preparation:

- **Targeted Study:** Develop a targeted study plan focusing on sections that are crucial for the companies you are applying to. For example, if a company emphasizes coding, ensure you are proficient in coding problems and techniques.
- **Holistic Approach:** While it's essential to excel in key areas, maintain a balanced approach to avoid neglecting other sections. Strong performance across all sections, combined with excellence in critical areas, enhances your overall candidacy.

Conclusion

Understanding how companies mark and declare results is vital for effective preparation. By focusing on the specific criteria that companies prioritize—whether it's sectional performance, overall scores, or GPA—you can tailor your preparation to meet their expectations. Adapting your strategy based on the role and the company's evaluation criteria will significantly improve your chances of success in the placement process.

In summary:

- **Focus on Key Sections:** Prioritize preparation for sections most relevant to the job role.
- **Maintain Overall Performance:** Ensure strong performance across all sections.
- **Align Preparation with Role Requirements:** Customize your study plan based on the job role's demands.

By aligning your preparation strategy with the specific evaluation criteria of each company, you can better navigate the placement process and enhance your prospects of securing a position.

6.7 How Do Companies Mark and Declare Results?

The process of marking and declaring results in campus placement tests involves several nuanced criteria that can vary from one company to another. Understanding these criteria is crucial for tailoring your preparation and improving your chances of success. Here's a detailed look at how companies handle marking and result declaration:

6.7.1 Criteria for Marking

1. Sectional Performance:

- **Importance of Specific Sections:** Companies often emphasize performance in specific sections that align with the job role. For example, a Data Analyst position will likely prioritize your performance in the Data Interpretation section over other areas.
- **Scoring Systems:** Tests may have sectional cutoffs or weightages where certain sections are given more importance based on the job profile. For instance, if a company values analytical skills highly, the analytical reasoning section might carry more weight in the final score.

2. Overall Performance:

- **Aggregate Scores:** In addition to sectional scores, companies may consider your overall performance. A strong overall score, combined with good performance in critical sections, can enhance your chances of moving forward in the selection process.
- **Cutoff Scores:** Some companies set an overall cutoff score that candidates must meet to be considered for further stages. These cutoffs can be influenced by the number of available positions and the overall performance of the candidates.

3. GPA Consideration:

- **Academic Performance:** Companies sometimes take your Grade Point Average (GPA) into account, especially if they use it as a tiebreaker or additional criterion. A higher GPA can sometimes compensate for lower performance in certain sections, though this varies by company.

6.7.2 How Results Are Declared
1. Results Based on Sectional Performance:

- **Targeted Evaluation:** For job roles requiring specific skills, companies might focus on performance in sections most relevant to the role. For example, if you're applying for a Data Analyst role, exceptional performance in Data Interpretation and related sections is crucial.
- **Sectional Cutoffs:** Companies may set cutoffs for individual sections. If you do not meet these cutoffs, you may not proceed to the next stage, regardless of your overall score.

2. Results Based on Overall Scores:

- **Comprehensive Evaluation:** In some cases, companies look at the total score and compare it against other candidates. High performance across all sections, even if not top in every section, can be a positive factor.
- **Ranking and Selection:** Candidates are often ranked based on their total scores. Those with higher rankings are more likely to be selected for interviews or further assessments.

3. Role-Specific Focus:

- **Customized Results:** Companies tailor their evaluation process based on the nature of the job. For example, IT companies that include coding questions may weigh coding performance heavily. If you perform well in other sections but poorly in coding, it might affect your overall selection.
- **Job Alignment:** Align your preparation with the job role. If the role requires strong analytical skills, focus on improving your performance in relevant sections. Companies are more likely to select candidates who align well with their job requirements.

6.7.3 Personal Experience Insights
1. Analyzing My Experience:

- **Capgemini Example:** Reflecting on my experience, my rejection in Capgemini's test was due to weak coding skills, despite performing well in other areas. This underscores the importance of focusing on all relevant sections, especially those critical to the job role.
- **Learning from Feedback:** Use feedback from previous tests to identify areas for improvement. If specific sections are emphasized, allocate more time to strengthen those areas.

2. Strategic Preparation:

- **Targeted Study:** Develop a targeted study plan focusing on sections that are crucial for the companies you are applying to. For example, if a company emphasizes coding, ensure you are proficient in coding problems and techniques.
- **Holistic Approach:** While it's essential to excel in key areas, maintain a balanced approach to avoid neglecting other sections. Strong performance across all sections, combined with excellence in critical areas, enhances your overall candidacy.

Conclusion

Understanding how companies mark and declare results is vital for effective preparation. By focusing on the specific criteria that companies prioritize—whether it's sectional performance, overall scores, or GPA—you can tailor your preparation to meet their expectations. Adapting your strategy based on the role and the company's evaluation criteria will significantly improve your chances of success in the placement process.

In summary:

- **Focus on Key Sections:** Prioritize preparation for sections most relevant to the job role.
- **Maintain Overall Performance:** Ensure strong performance across all sections.
- **Align Preparation with Role Requirements:** Customize your study plan based on the job role's demands.

By aligning your preparation strategy with the specific evaluation criteria of each company, you can better navigate the placement process and enhance your prospects of securing a position.

6.8 Company's Way of Selecting Candidates

The selection process for candidates during campus placements is often multifaceted and tailored to the specific needs of each company. Understanding how companies select candidates and preparing accordingly can significantly enhance your chances of success. Here's a comprehensive guide to navigating this process effectively, based on my experiences and observations.

1. Understanding Company-Specific Needs

1.1. Analyzing Past Trends:

- **Research:** Begin by researching the company's past recruitment trends. Look into the types of questions they have asked in previous interviews and the skills they prioritize. For instance, a Data Analyst role may focus heavily on data interpretation, case studies, and proficiency in tools like Excel.
- **Company Profile:** Tailor your preparation based on the company's profile and job requirements. If you're applying for a role that demands strong analytical skills, concentrate on practicing case studies, data analysis, and statistical tools relevant to the position.

1.2. Role-Specific Preparation:

- **Case Studies and Problem Solving:** For roles like Data Analysts, prepare for case studies that require you to analyze data, draw insights, and make recommendations. Practice solving real-world problems and presenting your findings clearly.
- **Technical Skills:** Brush up on technical skills pertinent to the role. For example, if Excel skills are crucial, ensure you are proficient in advanced functions, data manipulation, and creating complex reports.

2. Navigating the Interview Process

2.1. Preparing for Interviews:

- **Understand the Interview Structure:** Interviews may include a mix of technical questions, behavioral questions, and situational problems. Be prepared for each type and practice accordingly.
- **Behavioral and Situational Questions:** These are designed to assess how you handle real-world scenarios. Prepare by

reviewing common behavioral interview questions and reflecting on your past experiences to formulate structured responses using the STAR method (Situation, Task, Action, Result).

2.2. Handling Interview Pressure:

- **Practice and Simulate:** The pressure of the interview can sometimes lead to difficulties in answering questions you otherwise know well. Conduct mock interviews with peers or mentors to get used to the interview environment and pressure.
- **Stay Calm and Composed:** During the interview, if you find yourself under pressure, take a moment to collect your thoughts before responding. It's important to maintain composure to articulate your answers effectively.

3. *Balancing Technical and Non-Technical Skills*
3.1. Technical Knowledge:

- **Technical Proficiency:** While non-technical skills and soft skills are important, certain roles require a strong technical foundation. For instance, engineering roles might involve technical questions about concepts like Bending Moment and Shear Force Diagrams.
- **Practical Applications:** Sometimes, HRs or interviewers may focus more on practical problem-solving rather than theoretical knowledge. Be prepared to demonstrate your ability to apply technical concepts to solve real-world problems, even if you're not able to explain every theoretical aspect in detail.

3.2. Soft Skills and HR Interactions:

- **Effective Communication:** Demonstrate your ability to communicate effectively, both in terms of explaining technical concepts and discussing your experiences. Strong communication skills can leave a positive impression on the interviewers.

- **Convincing HRs:** In interviews with senior HR professionals, you might face situational or application-based questions where practical problem-solving is assessed. Use your common sense and logical reasoning to answer such questions effectively.

4. Drawing from Personal Experience
4.1. Learning from Past Interviews:

- **Reflect on Experiences:** Reflect on past interviews, like the one with L&T Heavy or Capgemini, to identify what went well and what didn't. For example, if you were rejected due to weaker coding skills, focus on improving these skills for future opportunities.
- **Adapt and Improve:** Use feedback from previous interviews to adapt your preparation strategy. If you faced challenges in explaining concepts, work on simplifying your explanations and practicing similar problems.

4.2. Balancing Preparation:

- **Holistic Approach:** While it's essential to focus on areas critical to the role, maintain a balanced approach. Ensure you have a solid grasp of both technical and non-technical aspects relevant to the job.
- **Preparation Strategy:** Develop a comprehensive preparation plan that includes technical skill enhancement, practice with real-world problems, and soft skills development.

5. Handling Different Types of Interviewers
5.1. Experienced vs. Junior HRs:

- **Senior HRs:** Experienced HR professionals may focus more on practical applications and situational questions. They might be more lenient with theoretical knowledge if you can demonstrate your problem-solving abilities effectively.

- **Junior HRs:** Junior HRs may emphasize theoretical knowledge and academic performance. Ensure you are well-prepared with the foundational concepts relevant to the role.

5.2. Adapting to Different Styles:

- **Tailored Responses:** Adjust your responses based on the interviewer's style. If faced with practical problems, focus on demonstrating your problem-solving approach rather than getting caught up in theoretical details.
- **Demonstrating Expertise:** For technical roles, be prepared to discuss and solve problems related to the job function. Show how your skills and knowledge can be applied to real-world scenarios relevant to the company.

Conclusion

Understanding how companies select candidates involves recognizing the nuances of their evaluation process and tailoring your preparation accordingly. By researching company-specific needs, preparing effectively for interviews, balancing technical and non-technical skills, and drawing from personal experience, you can enhance your chances of success.

In summary:

- **Research Company Needs:** Tailor your preparation based on the company's role-specific requirements.
- **Prepare for Interview Scenarios:** Practice handling different types of questions and maintain composure under pressure.
- **Balance Skills:** Develop both technical and soft skills, and be prepared for practical applications of your knowledge.
- **Adapt to Interviewers:** Adjust your responses based on the experience level and style of the interviewer.

By adopting a strategic approach and focusing on these areas, you can navigate the selection process more effectively and increase your likelihood of securing a position.

CHAPTER SEVEN

Analytics Quotient's Drive

1. Preparation and Initial Hurdles

The placement season for college students is often marked by a whirlwind of activities, anticipation, and challenges. For many, it's a critical time that can shape their future career paths. As students of NIT Manipur, we were eagerly preparing for various placement drives. Among the most anticipated was the drive conducted by L&T Heavy. However, this drive wasn't just about showcasing our skills; it was also a test of our logistical and financial planning.

Our journey began with organizing the logistics for the placement drive at NIT Nagaland. We needed to finalize a list of students interested in attending and arrange for transportation to ensure an early start the next morning. This required booking cabs and coordinating with our peers who were already at the NIT Nagaland campus. Despite our meticulous planning, some of us, including myself, found ourselves still on the NIT Silchar campus due to the ongoing L&T Heavy drive.

Staying away from home for several days involved managing expenses independently, which posed significant challenges. For students living on a tight budget, this was more than just a minor inconvenience. The cost of travel, food, and accommodation added up, creating financial stress. Our situation was further complicated by the lack of sufficient funds to purchase train tickets.

Although asking our parents for financial help was an option, we were hesitant. It wasn't about their willingness to assist but rather about our internal doubts and the fear of not meeting expectations.

We couldn't assure them of success, and this uncertainty made us reluctant to seek their support. Instead, we decided to manage with borrowed money and booked non-reserved train tickets. The train journey promised to be an ordeal, given the overcrowded conditions in general compartments.

2. The Train Journey: Challenges and Adaptations

Our train journey from Silchar to Dimapur was an experience in itself. The lack of reserved seats forced us to sit on the floor of the general compartment. Despite the discomfort, we tried to make the best of the situation. The train was packed with passengers, including many illegal immigrants, which further complicated our travel experience.

To cope with the lack of seating, we took turns sitting by the open doors to enjoy the fresh air and the rain. This moment of respite allowed us to appreciate the changing landscapes and the charm of the journey. To keep ourselves entertained, we played games on our mobile phones and chatted about various topics. The rain and the passing scenery created a picturesque setting, making the journey somewhat enjoyable despite the challenges.

We reached Lumding Station at 3:30 A.M., and the sight of the rainy weather did little to lift our spirits. Hunger was another concern, as we hadn't had a proper dinner. Fortunately, we managed to find a small food stall where we ordered dosas, which provided some much-needed comfort. We also had tea, snacks, and ice cream, which helped us pass the time while waiting for our connecting train.

The next leg of our journey was to Dimapur Station, which we reached by 7:00 A.M. We were immediately confronted with the challenge of negotiating with taxi drivers who demanded high fares. To avoid excessive costs, we decided to contact the T&P coordinators at NIT Nagaland, requesting them to arrange a bus for us. After a brief wait, the bus arrived, and we finally made our way to the NIT Nagaland campus.

3. Arrival and Campus Life

Upon arrival at NIT Nagaland, our first priority was to refresh ourselves. We had a hearty breakfast and took some time to relax. The campus was welcoming, and the fresh environment provided a sense of relief after the long journey. We took this opportunity to explore the campus and unwind.

Our plans included attending a movie in the nearby town. The film "GOLD" starring Akshay Kumar was playing, and we decided to watch it. Unfortunately, fatigue took its toll, and we struggled to stay awake during the movie. Despite our best efforts to enjoy the film, we found ourselves fighting sleep. The day ended with a satisfying dinner, and we went to bed early to prepare for the pre-placement session the following day.

4. The Pre-Placement Session and Test Preparation

The pre-placement session at NIT Nagaland was crucial in setting the stage for the upcoming tests. We were introduced to the format of the placement process and briefed on what to expect. This session included insights into the company's expectations, the nature of the tests, and the specific skills required.

The first round of the test began with an initial aptitude assessment designed to evaluate the reasoning and analytical skills of the candidates. Most of the questions focused on Data Interpretation, aligning with the company's goal of analyzing various types of data, including sales, distribution, and stock data from different clients. I managed to attempt a satisfactory number of questions, though the results weren't announced that day.

That evening, all my friends, feeling uncertain about their chances, decided to leave the NIT Nagaland campus. Only four of us remained, holding onto the hope of selection. The next morning, around 8:00 AM, my peaceful sleep was interrupted by a phone call to my friend's mobile. A local student informed him that he had been selected. Since this local student was only slightly acquainted with my friend, he mentioned that my name was likely on the list as well.

When the final list was shared, I was thrilled to discover that I had indeed been selected! Now, it was time to prepare for the second round of tests.

The second round of the test itself was centered around case study problems, which posed a significant challenge. These problems required us to analyze sales data and make recommendations to improve sales for a new product. The complexity of these problems meant that we had to think critically and apply our knowledge effectively.

I initially struggled with how to present my answers in a mathematical format. Observing my peers' detailed responses, which included graphs and extensive analysis, added to my anxiety. I was concerned that my approach might not meet the expectations of the evaluators.

5. Applying Engineering Knowledge

The case study round was designed to assess our problem-solving skills and analytical abilities through practical scenarios. One of the questions involved a company planning to introduce a new brand of products and required us to analyze sales data to propose strategies for enhancing the sales of this new brand. This type of problem was intended to test our ability to translate data analysis into actionable business strategies.

When faced with the first question, I found myself at a loss for how to approach it. The requirement to provide suggestions in a mathematical format was daunting, especially since I wasn't initially clear on how to structure my response. Observing my peers' solutions, which were laden with detailed graphs and complex analyses, only intensified my anxiety. Their advanced mathematical presentations made me question my own approach and capabilities.

I struggled internally with feelings of inadequacy, wondering why I couldn't think along similar lines. This self-doubt was a significant hurdle, as it affected my confidence and focus. Despite this, I resolved to overcome my fears and adopt a different strategy for tackling the problem.

Drawing upon my education in Industrial Engineering, I recalled a specific concept from the Inventory Control module that was highly relevant to the case study problem: the Price Model (Model No. 3). This model addresses how to optimize the purchase quantity of items based on different price ranges and discount structures.

The Price Model involves analyzing various price ranges associated with different quantities of items. The goal is to determine the optimal order quantity that minimizes the total cost, which includes holding costs, ordering costs, and purchase costs. This is particularly useful when suppliers offer discounts for bulk purchases, as it helps identify the quantity at which purchasing more items becomes more economical.

For instance, consider a scenario where a supplier offers a price of 90 Rs per piece for orders of less than 500 items, and 80 Rs per piece for orders of 500 or more. Using this model, we can calculate the total cost for both pricing options and determine the quantity at which the total cost is minimized. If the Economic Order Quantity (EOQ) is less than the quantity needed for the discount, the model helps decide whether to buy more to benefit from the lower price or to stick with the base price.

Successful Application and Reflection

Utilizing the Price Model allowed me to approach the case study with a structured methodology. Although I had only managed to solve the second question correctly, this application of engineering knowledge was pivotal in my selection for the final round. Being in the fourth position out of the four selected candidates was a testament to the value of leveraging technical knowledge, even when other areas might seem challenging.

This experience highlighted that even without extensive preparation in logical reasoning or additional study material, the application of core engineering principles can provide significant advantages. The satisfaction I felt knowing I had given my best effort in the selection process was invaluable. It underscored the importance of using one's specialized knowledge to navigate complex problems and achieve success.

Final Thoughts

Reflecting on the case study round, I realized that the integration of engineering concepts with practical problem-solving scenarios can significantly enhance performance. The experience reinforced the idea that thorough understanding and application of one's field of study can be crucial in overcoming challenges and making a lasting impression in competitive settings.

Even though the process was fraught with challenges, including initial doubts and the high-pressure environment of the selection process, I emerged with a greater appreciation for the role of engineering knowledge in real-world applications. The journey taught me that confidence, preparation, and the ability to adapt are key to succeeding in such demanding situations.

6. Overcoming Doubts and Achieving Selection

Despite my initial doubts about my performance, I was relieved to find my name on the final list of selected candidates for the second round. This success was a testament to the value of applying theoretical knowledge to practical problems.

The second round was another case study, and I continued to rely on my engineering background to navigate the challenges. My performance earned me a place in the final round, though I was in the fourth position out of the four students selected. This experience underscored the importance of applying one's knowledge and staying resilient, even when facing tough competition.

7. The Interview Round: Facing Personal Challenges

The interview round was a significant milestone, marking my first experience with a corporate interview. While waiting for the results of the second round, I had lunch and received a call from a friend confirming my selection. This news was both exciting and nerve-wracking, as it meant I was advancing to the final stage of the selection process.

The interview was a new and challenging experience. As an introvert, I found it difficult to cope with the pressure of facing an HR professional, especially given the lack of air conditioning and my visibly sweaty appearance. My nervousness affected my performance, and I struggled with even the most basic questions. The presence of a friendly and approachable HR lady did little to alleviate my anxiety, and my lack of confidence became evident.

8. Reflection and Learning

Despite the challenges and my performance in the interview, I took away valuable lessons from the experience. I realized that self-confidence and preparation are crucial in navigating placement drives and interviews. The experience taught me the importance of staying calm under pressure and being well-prepared for any situation.

My performance in the interview may not have been ideal, but I was determined to learn from the experience. I made a commitment to myself to approach future placement drives with greater confidence and preparation. I recognized that even if I didn't know all the answers, presenting myself with confidence and composure could make a significant difference.

9. Returning to College and Moving Forward

After the interviews, we booked bus tickets to return to our college. The journey back provided an opportunity for reflection and evaluation. I was determined to apply the lessons learned from this placement drive to future opportunities. The experience had taught me the value of perseverance, self-confidence, and the practical application of knowledge.

Returning to college, I continued to focus on improving my interview skills and preparing for future placement drives. I recognized that each experience, whether successful or not, contributed to my growth and development. The journey from NIT Silchar to NIT Nagaland was more than just a placement drive; it was a significant learning experience that shaped my approach to professional challenges.

10. Conclusion: The Journey of Growth and Learning

The journey through the placement drive, from the initial preparations to the final interview, was a transformative experience. It highlighted the importance of preparation, adaptability, and self-confidence in navigating the challenges of the placement process. Each phase of the journey, from managing logistics to facing interviews, contributed to my growth and understanding of the professional world.

In conclusion, the placement drive was not just about securing a job but also about personal and professional development. The experiences and lessons learned from this journey have equipped me with valuable insights and skills that will benefit me in future endeavors. The challenges faced and overcome during this process have reinforced the importance of resilience, confidence, and the application of knowledge in achieving success.

This detailed account of the journey from NIT Silchar to NIT Nagaland illustrates the complexities and challenges of the placement process. It serves as a reminder of the importance of preparation, adaptability, and self-belief in overcoming obstacles and seizing opportunities. The journey, with its highs and lows, ultimately contributed to my growth and readiness for future professional challenges.

The passage recounts the experiences of a student from NIT Silchar during the placement drive at NIT Nagaland. The preparation for the drive involved significant logistical and financial challenges, including arranging transportation and managing travel expenses. The journey by train was uncomfortable due to overcrowding, but the student and peers adapted by finding ways to stay positive and manage their situation.

Upon arriving at NIT Nagaland, the students focused on refreshing themselves and preparing for the pre-placement session. The placement process included case study problems that required mathematical and analytical skills. Initially, the student struggled with presenting solutions in a mathematical format but later applied knowledge from Industrial Engineering, specifically the Price Model from Inventory Control, to address the case study effectively.

Despite initial doubts and a challenging interview round marked by nervousness, the student successfully advanced through the selection process. The experience underscored the importance of preparation, self-confidence, and the application of academic knowledge in overcoming challenges. The student returned to college with valuable lessons on resilience and adaptability, highlighting the personal and professional growth achieved through the placement drive.

Message

The passage conveys several key messages:

1. **Preparation and Adaptability**: Effective preparation and adaptability are crucial in overcoming logistical and financial challenges during placement drives. Adapting to unexpected situations and managing stress can significantly impact the outcome.

2. **Application of Knowledge**: Applying academic knowledge to practical problems can provide a competitive edge. The use of the Price Model from Industrial Engineering in the case study illustrates how theoretical concepts can solve real-world issues.

3. **Self-Confidence and Resilience**: Confidence and resilience are vital for success, especially in high-pressure situations like interviews. Overcoming self-doubt and staying composed can make a significant difference in performance.

4. **Learning from Experience**: Each challenge and experience contributes to personal and professional growth. Reflecting on these experiences helps in improving future performance and preparing better for upcoming opportunities.

Overall, the passage highlights the journey of growth, the importance of applying knowledge, and the value of perseverance in achieving success.

CHAPTER EIGHT

Before I Could Take A Job!

Returning to our college, the atmosphere was one of palpable disarray. The initial enthusiasm that had marked the beginning of our journey had evaporated, leaving behind a sense of shattered hopes and crushed dedication. The future seemed uncertain and our spirits, once high, were now dwindling. It was evident that it was time to pause and reflect deeply on what had gone wrong. This period of reflection was not merely about assessing past failures but about recalibrating our approach to turn the tide in our favor.

We found ourselves in a dire situation. Nothing seemed to be aligning with our wishes, and control over the situation felt completely out of our grasp. Financial strain was a significant concern. We were spending money on the placement process, and the flow of expenses seemed relentless. We had no clear idea of how long this financial drain would continue or how intensely it would affect us throughout the placement journey.

However, a ray of hope emerged when our college, being a government institution, made a crucial announcement. The college promised to refund the expenses incurred for the placement drives, both those already spent and those to be spent in the future. This announcement brought a momentary relief and a renewed sense of optimism to our batch. We seized this opportunity and claimed the expenses for our entire batch, hoping it would alleviate some of our financial concerns until the placement process concluded.

Despite this financial reprieve, our spirits were still in shambles. The absence of company visits to our campus in the upcoming weeks exacerbated our frustration. We were drained, lacking the energy needed to re-engage with our goals. It was imperative for us to re-strategize and re-energize ourselves. We needed to scrutinize every theoretical concept to prepare effectively for the exams, cut out every possible distraction, and confine ourselves to our study spaces.

We faced a critical question: Were we ready to commit ourselves fully to this renewed effort? If the answer was 'yes', then success was within our reach. Some of our classmates were disengaged from the recruitment process, which only served to undermine our collective confidence. Yet, we focused on our own path, driven by the need to prove ourselves to our parents. Gaining their trust and support was essential not just for our immediate goals but also for our future aspirations, including the possibility of joining coaching institutes for competitive exams post-graduation.

In contemplating the future, I faced a dilemma: if I secured a position with an MNC, I would need to make a critical decision—whether to stay and build a career with the firm or leave to prepare for central government PSU exams. To avoid this uncertainty, I dedicated myself to focusing on strategies and concepts that would guarantee at least one job offer before graduating. I approached this with renewed vigor, pushing myself harder than before.

My confidence grew as I began scoring better in test series. However, the placement papers presented challenges, as there were no previous year papers available online, making it difficult to gauge strengths and weaknesses. I focused on covering essential topics in Quantitative Aptitude and Reasoning, which gave me a slight edge over others. This preparation was crucial as it set the foundation for my improved performance.

The next significant test was with L&T Construction, following several unsuccessful attempts with other recruiting companies. The pressure was immense. As we approached the end of our college life, the urgency to secure a job became even more critical. The prospect of returning home without a job loomed large, and the potential judgment from family and acquaintances was daunting. I envisioned the harsh words and disapproving comments that would follow if I failed. This pressure fueled my determination to succeed.

Fortunately, I managed to secure an offer letter from L&T Construction by the end. Securing this position was not straightforward; it involved overcoming numerous hurdles. The challenge was not only to perform well in interviews but also to face the reality of not securing a job despite making significant efforts. The fear of being labeled a failure despite doing well in various selection rounds was a constant struggle.

The most challenging aspect was communicating my status to my parents and other important people in my life. Their doubts and judgments were difficult to handle, but it was essential to maintain focus on our studies and not let these external pressures deter us. We realized that the only way to move forward was to concentrate on our preparation and address our weak areas.

Our preparation involved revisiting fundamental concepts, studying deeply, and practicing Aptitude questions from mocks and previous years. This focused effort over the course of a month began to yield positive results. Confidence levels increased, and the feeling of being better prepared became evident.

Then, L&T Construction showed interest in our college for a placement drive, which was scheduled to take place at NIT Silchar. Traveling from our college, NIT Manipur, to NIT Silchar was no small feat. The journey was challenging due to the hilly roads, and additional complications arose when we learned about a "Bandh" in Manipur. This local protest disrupted our plans, and despite efforts to find alternative solutions, we ultimately had to forgo the drive.

Recognizing the critical nature of this opportunity, we devised a plan to convince the HR of L&T to arrange a separate placement drive for us. After persistent discussions with our college management and HR, we successfully negotiated for a separate drive. The new dates were set, and the location was decided—NIT Sikkim. Despite these confirmations, the lack of certainty about the drive's occurrence and our initial reluctance to fully commit to preparation created a lingering sense of hesitation.

The realization that the drive was indeed happening gradually set in, and our preparation intensified. We confirmed our participation, provided necessary details, and received our system-generated resumes, which were to be carried to the exam center as an admit card. This process underscored the importance of hope and commitment. Despite knowing the dates and location, maintaining a hopeful attitude was crucial for sustained motivation and effective preparation.

The journey to NIT Sikkim was marked by both physical and emotional challenges. Yet, our preparation paid off, and the drive itself was a testament to the power of hope and determination. Challenges, as we experienced, are not meant to break us but to reveal our true potential. Embracing and overcoming these challenges allowed us to tap into our inner strength and achieve our goals.

In the end, the experience taught us that success requires more than just effort; it demands resilience, adaptability, and a positive mindset. The journey was fraught with obstacles, but by maintaining hope, staying focused, and pushing through difficulties, we managed to secure a position and prove our capabilities. The entire process, from the financial struggles to the final placement, highlighted the transformative power of perseverance and self-belief.

Several valuable takeaways that can be applied broadly to personal and professional challenges, have also been discussed here. Here's a detailed breakdown of the key lessons:

1. Reflection and Adaptation

Takeaway: Regularly pausing to reflect on what is not working and being willing to adapt your strategies is crucial for overcoming obstacles.

Explanation: The narrative begins with a period of reflection where the protagonist and their peers assess their failures and strategize for improvement. This moment of introspection and willingness to change their approach was essential for making progress. It emphasizes the importance of being flexible and responsive to evolving circumstances rather than persisting with ineffective methods.

2. Financial Management and Support

Takeaway: Having a support system and financial management strategies in place can provide relief during challenging times.

Explanation: The announcement from the college about refunding placement-related expenses provided significant relief and allowed students to focus on their preparation without the added stress of financial burdens. This highlights the importance of seeking and utilizing available support systems to manage stress and maintain focus during difficult times.

3. Renewed Effort and Focus

Takeaway: When facing setbacks, doubling down on effort and focusing on core strengths can lead to improved outcomes.

Explanation: After the initial failure and lack of progress, the protagonist renewed their commitment with greater intensity. They concentrated on fundamental concepts and practice, which enhanced their performance. This underscores the importance of recommitting to your goals with renewed vigor and concentrating on areas that can offer the greatest benefit.

4. Handling Failure and External Judgments

Takeaway: Resilience in the face of failure and dealing with external judgments constructively is vital for long-term success.

Explanation: The protagonist faced multiple failures and harsh judgments from others, including potential criticism from family. Despite this, they maintained their focus and continued to strive for success. This lesson highlights the importance of resilience and the ability to ignore detractors while staying committed to one's goals.

5. Effective Preparation and Time Management

Takeaway: Proper preparation and managing your time effectively are essential for achieving success in competitive scenarios.

Explanation: The protagonist's improved performance was a result of thorough preparation and effective time management.

They practiced consistently, studied deeply, and prepared for the placement drive, which ultimately led to success. This reinforces the value of disciplined preparation and strategic time management.

6. Proactive Problem Solving

Takeaway: Taking initiative to solve problems and seek alternatives can turn potential setbacks into opportunities.

Explanation: When faced with the "Bandh" that prevented them from attending the placement drive at NIT Silchar, the students proactively sought to arrange an alternative drive at NIT Sikkim. This proactive approach not only saved the opportunity but also demonstrated the importance of taking initiative and problem-solving under pressure.

7. Maintaining Hope and Motivation

Takeaway: Keeping hope alive and staying motivated, even when faced with uncertainty, is crucial for achieving success.

Explanation: Despite knowing the drive's dates and location, the initial reluctance and lack of belief in its occurrence were obstacles. It was only by maintaining hope and progressively intensifying their preparation that they overcame this challenge. This underscores the importance of hope and persistent motivation in achieving one's goals.

8. Importance of Self-Belief

Takeaway: Believing in your abilities and potential is a fundamental aspect of overcoming challenges and achieving success.

Explanation: Throughout the narrative, despite setbacks and difficulties, the protagonist's self-belief and determination were key factors in their eventual success. This lesson highlights that self-belief is crucial for persisting through challenges and reaching one's objectives.

9. The Role of Support Networks

Takeaway: Leveraging support networks, including friends, family, and institutional support, can be instrumental in navigating difficult situations.

Explanation: The support from the college, peers, and family played a significant role in the protagonist's journey. Building and utilizing a strong support network can provide necessary resources, encouragement, and practical assistance when facing challenges.

10. Embracing Challenges as Growth Opportunities

Takeaway: Challenges should be viewed as opportunities for growth rather than obstacles to success.

Explanation: The various challenges faced, from financial issues to placement drive complications, were reframed as opportunities for personal and professional growth. This perspective helped the protagonist to navigate difficulties more effectively and ultimately achieve their goals.

These takeaways provide valuable insights into handling adversity, managing stress, and achieving success through resilience, preparation, and support.

Obstacles and Solutions for the author as a final year student facing placement exams:

1. Shattered Hope and Dwindling Dedication

Obstacle:

- Returning to college, the initial enthusiasm had vanished, leaving students feeling disheartened and uncertain about the future.

Solution:

- **Pause and Reflect:** Take time to analyze past efforts and identify what went wrong. Reflect on achievements and setbacks to gain clarity on how to move forward.
- **Recalibrate Approach:** Adjust strategies based on the reflection to rekindle motivation and dedication. Set specific, achievable goals to regain focus and enthusiasm.

2. Financial Strain

Obstacle:

- Continuous spending on placement processes created a financial burden, causing stress and uncertainty about future expenses.

Solution:

- **Utilize Financial Support:** Make use of any available financial aid or reimbursements offered by the college. In this case, the college's promise to refund placement expenses alleviated some financial pressure.
- **Budget Wisely:** Plan and monitor spending carefully to manage financial resources effectively. Create a budget to track and control expenses related to placement activities.

3. Lack of Company Visits and Absence of Energy
Obstacle:

- No immediate company visits led to frustration and a lack of energy among students, making it difficult to re-engage with preparation.

Solution:

- **Re-Strategize and Re-Energize:** Develop a new study plan and allocate specific times for preparation. Avoid distractions and create a focused study environment to boost productivity.
- **Set Short-Term Goals:** Break down preparation into smaller, manageable tasks to regain motivation and maintain momentum.

4. Disengagement from Classmates
Obstacle:

- Some classmates were not participating in the recruitment process, which negatively affected collective morale and confidence.

Solution:

- **Focus on Personal Goals:** Concentrate on individual objectives and self-improvement rather than being influenced by others' attitudes.
- **Seek Support and Motivation:** Find encouragement from peers who are also dedicated to the process. Form study groups or seek mentorship for additional support.

5. Decision Dilemma Between Job and Further Preparation

Obstacle:

- Uncertainty about whether to accept a job offer from an MNC or pursue further preparation for central government exams.

Solution:

- **Strategic Focus:** Prioritize obtaining at least one job offer before making career decisions. This provides a safety net and reduces pressure.
- **Explore Options Early:** Research and prepare for alternative career paths or further studies while actively seeking job offers.

6. Lack of Previous Year Papers and Difficulty in Assessment

Obstacle:

- Absence of previous year placement papers made it challenging to assess strengths and weaknesses and gauge preparation needs.

Solution:

- **Focus on Core Topics:** Concentrate on essential areas such as Quantitative Aptitude and Reasoning, which are commonly tested.

- **Use Mock Tests:** Practice with mock tests and sample questions to simulate the exam environment and identify areas for improvement.

7. Navigating Physical and Emotional Challenges
Obstacle:

- Difficulties such as the "Bandh" disrupting travel plans and the emotional strain of nearing the end of college life.

Solution:

- **Develop Contingency Plans:** Have backup plans for travel and other logistical issues. Stay informed about potential disruptions and plan alternatives in advance.
- **Maintain Emotional Resilience:** Use stress-management techniques and stay positive despite challenges. Seek support from friends, family, or counselors if needed.

8. Pressure of Securing a Job and Facing Judgments
Obstacle:

- The pressure to secure a job and fear of judgment from family and acquaintances if unsuccessful.

Solution:

- **Build Confidence:** Strengthen self-belief and focus on your strengths and preparation efforts. Prepare thoroughly to improve performance and confidence.
- **Communicate Effectively:** Be open and honest with family about your progress and challenges. Share your plans and efforts to gain their understanding and support.

9. Uncertainty About Placement Drive and Procrastination

Obstacle:

- Uncertainty about the placement drive's occurrence led to procrastination and lack of commitment to preparation.

Solution:

- **Commit to Preparation:** Stay committed to your study plan and maintain consistent preparation, regardless of uncertainties. Set firm deadlines and stick to them.
- **Monitor Progress:** Track your preparation progress and adjust strategies as needed to stay on course.

10. Overcoming Obstacles in Placement Drive Execution
Obstacle:

- Difficulties in organizing and participating in the placement drive due to logistical issues and initial reluctance.

Solution:

- **Coordinate with College Management:** Work closely with college authorities and HR to ensure smooth organization of placement drives.
- **Prepare Thoroughly:** Ensure all required documentation and preparations are completed well in advance of the placement drive.

By addressing these obstacles with the suggested solutions, final-year students can improve their preparation and increase their chances of securing a placement successfully. Maintaining resilience, focus, and effective time management is key to navigating the challenges of the placement process

Message from the Passage: Overcoming Challenges in Placement Exams:

The journey through final-year placements can be fraught with various obstacles, but with the right approach and mindset, these challenges can be navigated effectively. Here are the core messages distilled from the passage about overcoming these challenges:

1. **Embrace Reflection and Adaptation:**

   - **Message:** When faced with shattered hopes and dwindling dedication, it's crucial to pause and reflect on past efforts. Assess what went wrong and adjust your approach accordingly. This reflective practice helps rekindle motivation and enables you to set realistic, achievable goals to regain your focus and enthusiasm.

2. **Manage Financial Strain Wisely:**

   - **Message:** Financial concerns can be a significant burden during placement preparations. Utilize any available financial aid or reimbursements to alleviate the strain. Additionally, budgeting wisely and planning your expenses carefully can help manage financial resources effectively and reduce stress.

3. **Re-Energize and Re-Strategize:**

   - **Message:** Lack of company visits and dwindling energy can lead to frustration. Develop a new study plan and set short-term goals to maintain motivation. Creating a focused and distraction-free study environment can significantly boost productivity and help you stay on track.

4. **Focus on Personal Growth:**

   - **Message:** Disengagement from classmates or negative collective morale can impact your confidence. Focus on your personal goals and seek motivation from peers who are also dedicated. Forming study groups or seeking mentorship can provide additional support and encouragement.

5. **Navigate Career Decisions Strategically:**

    ◦ **Message:** The dilemma between accepting a job offer or pursuing further preparation requires careful consideration. Prioritize securing at least one job offer as a safety net. Explore and prepare for alternative career paths or further studies to keep your options open.

6. **Adapt to Assessment Challenges:**

    ◦ **Message:** When faced with a lack of previous year papers or difficulty in assessing preparation needs, focus on core topics such as Quantitative Aptitude and Reasoning. Use mock tests and sample questions to simulate the exam environment and identify areas for improvement.

7. **Develop Resilience for Physical and Emotional Challenges:**

    ◦ **Message:** Obstacles such as travel disruptions or emotional strain require resilience. Develop contingency plans for logistical issues and maintain a positive mindset despite challenges. Seek support from friends, family, or counselors to manage stress effectively.

8. **Build Confidence and Communicate Effectively:**

    ◦ **Message:** The pressure to secure a job and fear of judgment can be overwhelming. Strengthen your self-belief by focusing on your strengths and thorough preparation. Openly communicate with family about your progress and challenges to gain their understanding and support.

9. **Combat Procrastination with Commitment:**

    ◦ **Message:** Uncertainty about placement drives can lead to procrastination. Commit to your study plan and maintain consistent preparation, regardless of uncertainties. Set firm deadlines and monitor your progress to stay on course.

10. **Overcome Logistical Challenges with Preparation:**

    ◦ **Message:** Difficulties in organizing and participating in placement drives require effective coordination. Work closely with college management and HR to ensure smooth organization. Prepare all necessary documentation and requirements well in advance to avoid last-minute issues.

Overall Message: The key to successfully navigating the final year placement process lies in resilience, effective planning, and maintaining a positive mindset. By addressing obstacles proactively and employing strategic solutions, students can enhance their preparation, overcome challenges, and significantly improve their chances of securing a successful placement.

CHAPTER NINE

The Final Journey Of My College

As the dates for the placement drive at NIT Sikkim approached, the anticipation was palpable. For us, the students of NIT Manipur, this was more than just a routine event; it was our last opportunity to secure a job before graduation. The urgency of the situation was undeniable, as there were no signs of other companies planning to visit our campus in the near future. The pressure was on, and it became clear that we needed to perform flawlessly if we hoped to land a job offer.

The preparation was intense. Days and nights were spent poring over notes, revising concepts, and honing our interview skills. Every piece of information was scrutinized, every formula and theory was reviewed, and mock interviews were conducted to simulate the real experience. The goal was singular: to be fully prepared for the placement drive at NIT Sikkim.

The logistics of the trip added another layer of complexity. Traveling from Imphal to Ravangla, where NIT Sikkim is located, was no small feat. NIT Manipur, nestled amidst the hills, is not easily accessible. We had two primary options for leaving Imphal: by air or by road. Given our budget constraints, flying was not a feasible option. The decision was made; we would travel by road.

The roads from Imphal to Guwahati are known for their challenging terrain. They wind through steep hills and often feature sharp, hairpin turns. The journey by road is infamous for inducing motion sickness among travelers. This knowledge did little to ease our apprehensions, but we pressed on. We chose to travel by "winger," a type of four-wheeler that offers more seating than vehicles like the Mahindra Scorpio or Bolero but fewer seats than a bus. These vehicles are well-suited for hilly roads due to their powerful engines and rugged design.

Our journey began early in the morning. We boarded the winger at around 8 a.m., ready for the long haul to Guwahati. The ride was uncomfortable and tiring, but the real challenge lay ahead. We reached Guwahati Railway Station by around 6 p.m., exhausted but relieved to have completed the first leg of our journey.

After a quick dinner at a nearby restaurant, we prepared for the next phase: traveling to NJP Railway Station. This part of the journey was equally taxing. We had to endure a long, uncomfortable train ride in second-class seats, which was a far cry from the comfort we had hoped for. The lack of proper rest and the cramped conditions made the journey even more grueling.

Upon arriving at NJP Railway Station the following morning, we faced another challenge: how to reach Ravangla. Our initial plan was to catch a direct bus, but our timing was unfortunate. The day of our arrival coincided with Vishwakarma Pooja, a significant festival in the Hindu calendar. This festival, observed primarily in industrial and manufacturing sectors, often results in reduced public transportation options. Consequently, we found it difficult to locate a direct bus to Ravangla.

Undeterred, we opted for a longer route involving multiple vehicle changes. We first took a winger, then a sumo, followed by another type of vehicle, each transition adding to the complexity of our journey. The trip was exhausting, and by the time we reached Ravangla, it was around 6 or 7 p.m. We were physically drained and eager to find accommodation.

Our initial hope was to stay in the NIT Sikkim hostel, but our plans were thwarted by the lack of available space. With no other immediate options, we sought refuge in a local hotel. The hotel staff informed us that the rate was Rs. 400 per night, a rate we had no choice but to accept given our circumstances. We were relieved to have a place to stay but were too tired to explore or enjoy the surroundings.

The following day was packed with significant events. We had exams and interviews lined up, and despite our fatigue, we needed to stay sharp. Some of us tried to review concepts and solve problems, while others sought rest. My friend and I engaged in mock interviews, testing each other's knowledge and analytical skills. Our goal was to ensure we were as prepared as possible for the impending interview.

The night before the exam and interview was particularly trying. Our hotel room was cold, and the lack of proper heating made it difficult to get comfortable. We rose early, shivering in the chilly air, and prepared to head to the exam venue. Despite our exhaustion and the uncomfortable conditions, we had no choice but to proceed with the day's events.

At the exam venue, we were faced with another challenge: the systems for the exam were not ready on time. We waited anxiously as the systems were set up, knowing that every minute of delay increased our stress. When the exam finally started, it lasted for about 90 minutes. We poured our efforts into answering questions, hoping to make a strong impression.

After the exam, we anxiously awaited the results. The tension was palpable, and we hoped for an announcement before we left the venue. However, the results were not declared until lunchtime, forcing us to return to our hotel rooms empty-handed.

While we were waiting, an unexpected call from an unknown number added to our anxiety. One of my friends answered, and it turned out to be the T&P coordinator. He informed us that the results had been announced and began listing the names of selected candidates. My heart raced as he read through the names, and I could hardly contain my nervousness. When my name was finally announced, a wave of relief and joy washed over me.

It was time for the much-anticipated interview round, which consisted of three key components: a technical assessment, an HR interview, and an extempore session. On the day of the interviews, I arrived at the venue filled with a mix of excitement and nerves. However, as the hours passed, it became evident that the HR team had not yet arrived. We waited outside the hall, chatting with fellow candidates and exchanging nervous glances as the afternoon wore on.

Finally, around 7:00 or 8:00 PM, the interviewers arrived, and the atmosphere shifted from anxious anticipation to focused determination. The interviews commenced in various sections of the hall, with candidates being called in one by one. As I waited for my turn, I observed the interactions between my peers and the interviewers, trying to glean any insights into the types of questions being asked.

When my name was called, I took a deep breath and stepped into the room. I greeted the panel warmly, and they reciprocated with friendly smiles. The HR portion began with some standard questions: "Tell me about yourself," "What does your father do?" and "Where are you from, and what's special about your hometown?" I answered confidently, sharing relevant details about my background, interests, and experiences. I emphasized my passion for learning and my motivation for applying to this position, hoping to make a good impression.

Once the HR questions were completed, the panel transitioned to the technical round. This part of the interview was crucial, and I felt the weight of it as they began firing questions at me. They probed into concepts like Pascal's Law and Bernoulli's Principle, both of which I had studied extensively. I answered questions about gear systems, the laws of thermodynamics, and the various types of gears used in mechanical applications. They also challenged me with numerical problems related to these topics, and I was pleased to find that I could tackle nearly all of them with clarity and confidence.

After the technical round, it was time for the extempore session. I was asked to choose a topic from a cup filled with prompts, each representing a different theme. When I drew my topic, "Sustainable

Development," I felt a surge of excitement. I quickly organized my thoughts and spoke passionately for about two minutes, addressing the importance of balancing economic growth with environmental stewardship and social equity. Just as I was gaining momentum, the panel asked me to conclude my thoughts, signaling the end of my interview.

Although it felt relatively brief, the entire interview lasted about 20 to 25 minutes. While I couldn't recall every question they had asked, I remembered the key themes and topics that had been discussed. It was an enriching experience, and I felt a sense of accomplishment as I left the interview room.

Once the interviews concluded, I joined my fellow candidates and we collectively left the NIT Sikkim campus, heading back to our accommodations. Reflecting on the day's events, I felt a mix of relief and optimism, knowing I had given my best effort and learned a great deal throughout the process.

As we concluded this phase of the journey, we took the opportunity to explore Sikkim. We visited several famous places, appreciating the beauty of the region despite the exhaustion. Eventually, we prepared to leave and head back to our hostels.

Our journey took us to Bagdogra Airport in West Bengal. After the exhausting trip from Ravangla to Bagdogra, we decided to stay in a hotel to recuperate. While relaxing, I received a message from our TPO in a WhatsApp group. The message included the names of selected candidates from the interview. My heart raced as I scrolled through the notification, hoping to see my name. Finally, upon opening the message, I saw my name among the selected students. It was a moment of profound happiness and relief.

The selection was not only a personal achievement but also a moment of immense satisfaction for my parents, who had high hopes for my success.

The experience of this journey was a powerful lesson in perseverance and determination. It demonstrated that both success and failure are integral to life, but what truly matters is how you maintain focus and resolve. Even when the path seemed uncertain, having a clear vision and strong motivation guided me through the challenges. The journey was arduous, but it underscored the importance of staying dedicated and believing in oneself.

This journey taught me that the process of selection and rejection is a natural part of life. What matters most is how you stay determined and focused, regardless of the challenges you face. The experience reinforced the importance of having a clear vision and understanding your motivations. Success becomes achievable when you are clear about your goals and maintain dedication throughout the journey.

From the passage, several key takeaways emerge, each offering valuable insights into personal development, perseverance, and preparation. Here's a summary of the takeaways:

1. Importance of Preparation

- **Thorough Preparation:** Rigorous preparation is crucial for success. The detailed review of notes, mock interviews, and revising concepts before the placement drive illustrate the importance of being well-prepared for any significant challenge.
- **Adaptability:** Being adaptable in your preparation—adjusting strategies based on the situation—can greatly enhance your performance.

2. Dealing with Challenges

- **Overcoming Obstacles:** The journey to NIT Sikkim involved numerous challenges, from difficult travel conditions to inadequate accommodation. Overcoming these obstacles required resilience and problem-solving skills.
- **Handling Adversity:** Facing and managing unexpected issues, such as the reduced availability of transportation due to a festival, highlights the need to remain flexible and proactive in problem-solving.

3. Managing Stress and Fatigue

- **Coping with Exhaustion:** The experience emphasizes the importance of managing stress and fatigue, particularly when dealing with physically and mentally draining situations.
- **Effective Rest:** Proper rest and managing sleep during critical periods can impact performance. The passage underscores the struggle to stay focused despite exhaustion.

4. Value of Persistence and Determination

- **Continuous Effort:** Persistent effort in the face of setbacks, such as the multiple vehicle changes and long journeys, demonstrates the value of staying committed to your goals.
- **Inner Drive:** Determination and a clear understanding of your motivation can help you overcome significant challenges and achieve your objectives.

5. Significance of Emotional Resilience

- **Handling Anxiety:** The anxiety and nervousness experienced before receiving the results and during the interview highlight the importance of emotional resilience.
- **Embracing Success and Failure:** Understanding that both success and failure are part of life's journey helps in managing expectations and maintaining a positive outlook.

6. Learning from Experience

- **Reflection:** Reflecting on the journey provides insights into personal growth and areas for improvement. Each experience, whether positive or negative, contributes to your overall development.
- **Life Lessons:** The journey teaches that success is not just about achieving goals but also about the lessons learned and the growth experienced along the way.

7. Planning and Execution

- **Strategic Planning:** Effective planning for both the journey and the placement drive is crucial. The passage shows how detailed planning and execution can significantly impact the outcome.
- **Flexibility in Plans:** Being prepared to alter plans based on real-time situations, such as finding alternative transportation, is essential for navigating complex situations.

8. Gratitude and Humility

- **Appreciating Support:** The support from family and the relief of achieving success highlight the importance of appreciating and acknowledging the support system around you.
- **Humility in Success:** Despite the success, remaining humble and acknowledging the role of perseverance and preparation in achieving your goals is crucial.

9. Future Outlook

- **Continuous Improvement:** The passage sets the stage for future parts of the book, focusing on ongoing development and adaptation in a corporate environment and government job preparation.
- **Growth Mindset:** Embracing a mindset focused on growth and learning from each experience prepares you for future challenges and opportunities.

In essence, the passage illustrates a comprehensive journey filled with preparation, challenges, and eventual success, underscoring key life lessons about perseverance, resilience, and the importance of staying focused on one's goals.

Motivational Message from the story:

"Determination and perseverance can transform seemingly insurmountable challenges into stepping stones toward success.

The journey may be arduous, but with preparation, resilience, and a clear vision, you can overcome obstacles and achieve your goals."

Detailed Explanation

1. Determination and Perseverance

Meaning:

- **Determination** refers to the firm resolution to achieve something despite difficulties or delay in achieving success.
- **Perseverance** is the continuous effort to do or achieve something despite difficulties, failure, or opposition.

Explanation: In the context of the passage, the journey from Imphal to NIT Sikkim was fraught with challenges, from difficult travel conditions to unexpected delays. The story illustrates how determination and perseverance are critical in navigating such obstacles. The author and their peers faced significant hurdles, including long and uncomfortable travel, lack of accommodation, and challenging exam conditions. Despite these difficulties, their unwavering resolve to succeed and secure a job propelled them forward.

Example:

- The decision to travel by a winger despite its discomfort, the effort to revise thoroughly despite the exhaustion, and the persistence to manage travel disruptions reflect the essence of determination and perseverance.

2. Transforming Challenges into Stepping Stones

Meaning:

- **Challenges** are difficulties that arise during the pursuit of goals.
- **Stepping stones** are incremental achievements or milestones that help you progress towards a larger goal.

Explanation: The story demonstrates how the challenges encountered were not just obstacles but opportunities for growth. Each difficulty, such as the lack of direct transportation or the uncomfortable train journey, was a stepping stone that contributed to their eventual success. By tackling each issue head-on and adapting their strategies, the author and his subordinates used these challenges to build resilience and improve their readiness.

Example:

- The inconvenience of changing multiple vehicles due to a festival became a lesson in adaptability and problem-solving. Similarly, the discomfort of the second-class train seats highlighted the need for mental strength and endurance.

3. *The Importance of Preparation*
Meaning:

- **Preparation** involves thorough planning and readiness for potential challenges before they arise.

Explanation: The passage underscores that success is not merely a result of seizing opportunities but also of being prepared for them. The detailed preparation before the placement drive—revising notes, conducting mock interviews, and strategizing for the journey—was pivotal. Preparation helps you anticipate and mitigate potential issues, ensuring you are well-equipped to handle unforeseen challenges.

Example:

- The effort to prepare for the exam and interview, despite the difficult conditions, exemplifies how thorough preparation can influence outcomes positively.

4. *Resilience in the Face of Adversity*
Meaning:

- **Resilience** is the capacity to recover quickly from difficulties and adapt to adversity.

Explanation: The story also illustrates the importance of resilience—maintaining a positive attitude and continuing to strive towards your goals even when faced with setbacks. The students' ability to endure long journeys, cope with fatigue, and stay focused on their goal of securing a job is a testament to their resilience. Resilience allows individuals to bounce back from difficulties and continue moving forward, turning potential failures into successes.
Example:

- The exhaustion from travel and the discomfort during the journey were significant challenges, yet the students persisted, demonstrating resilience by staying committed to their goal despite the adversities.

5. Having a Clear Vision
Meaning:

- **Clear Vision** involves having a defined goal and understanding the reasons behind pursuing it.

Explanation: The story highlights that having a clear vision is crucial for maintaining motivation and direction. The students' clarity about their goal—to secure a job—provided them with the motivation to persevere through difficulties. A clear vision helps in setting priorities, making strategic decisions, and staying focused on what matters most.
Example:

- The focus on the placement drive and the understanding of its importance as a critical opportunity for employment drove the students to overcome various obstacles.

Conclusion

The motivational message from the passage is a powerful reminder that with determination and perseverance, challenges can be transformed into opportunities for growth and success. Preparation, resilience, and a clear vision are essential elements in navigating difficult paths and achieving one's goals. The journey described in the passage serves as an inspiring example of how these qualities can lead to success even in the face of significant obstacles.

The second part of this book will delve into my experiences working in a corporate office, exploring the various challenges I faced in day-to-day work and the reasons behind my decision to resign and pursue competitive government exams. **The third part** will cover my preparation for government jobs and offer insights into the work-life balance in government offices. I hope my readers find the upcoming sections as engaging and insightful as this journey.

Part-2

This section explores the dynamics of working in corporate offices, providing insights into performance reviews, work-life balance, and workplace culture as below:

1. Working Style of Corporate Offices

Corporate offices, particularly in multinational companies (MNCs), often operate with a structured, formal working style. This environment is characterized by:

- **Hierarchical Structure:** Corporate offices typically have a clear chain of command, with defined roles and responsibilities at each level. This hierarchy ensures that decision-making processes are systematic and that responsibilities are well-distributed.
- **Standardized Processes:** MNCs often implement standardized processes and procedures to maintain consistency across global operations. This includes uniformity in project management, communication protocols, and reporting practices.
- **Goal-Oriented Approach:** Corporate workplaces are generally focused on achieving specific business objectives. This goal-oriented approach drives performance and productivity, with employees expected to contribute to the company's targets and strategic goals.
- **Formal Communication:** Communication in corporate settings is usually formal, with a preference for written reports, emails, and official meetings. This formality helps in maintaining professionalism and ensures that important information is documented and accessible.

2. Performance Review System

Performance reviews in MNCs are typically rigorous and structured, designed to evaluate employees' contributions, skills, and potential for growth. Key elements include:

- **Regular Evaluations:** Performance reviews are often conducted annually or semi-annually. These evaluations assess employees' achievements against pre-set objectives and key performance indicators (KPIs).
- **360-Degree Feedback:** Many MNCs use a 360-degree feedback system, where employees receive performance feedback from peers, subordinates, and supervisors. This comprehensive approach provides a well-rounded view of an individual's performance.
- **Objective Metrics:** Reviews are based on objective metrics such as project outcomes, sales targets, or productivity measures. This quantitative approach ensures that evaluations are fair and aligned with business goals.
- **Development Plans:** Post-evaluation, employees typically receive feedback on their strengths and areas for improvement. Based on this feedback, development plans are created to address skill gaps and enhance career growth.
- **Promotion and Compensation:** Performance reviews often impact promotion decisions and compensation adjustments. High performers are generally rewarded with promotions, salary increases, or bonuses, whereas underperformers may face corrective actions or developmental programs.

3. Work-Life Balance

Work-life balance in corporate offices can vary significantly depending on the company's culture and the role. General aspects include:

- **Long Working Hours:** Corporate jobs, especially in high-pressure roles, may require long working hours and occasional overtime. This can impact personal time and lead to a challenging work-life balance.
- **Flexible Work Options:** Some MNCs offer flexible working arrangements, such as remote work or flexible hours, to support employees' work-life balance. However, the availability of such options often depends on the company's policies and the nature of the job.
- **Stress Management:** High-stress environments are common in corporate settings, particularly in competitive roles. Companies may offer stress management resources, such as wellness programs or counseling services, to help employees cope with workplace pressure.
- **Cultural Expectations:** In some corporate cultures, there is a strong emphasis on work commitment, which can blur the lines between work and personal life. This cultural expectation can affect employees' ability to disconnect and maintain a healthy balance.

4. Work Culture and Personality Development

The work culture in corporate offices can significantly influence employees' personality development. Factors to consider include:

- **Professional Growth:** A supportive work culture that encourages continuous learning and development can positively impact personality growth. Opportunities for training, mentorship, and skill-building can enhance employees' confidence and capabilities.
- **Networking Opportunities:** Working in a corporate environment provides chances to build professional networks and relationships. Interacting with diverse teams and

stakeholders can broaden employees' perspectives and improve interpersonal skills.

- **Feedback and Recognition:** Constructive feedback and recognition play a crucial role in personality development. Positive reinforcement and acknowledgment of achievements can boost morale and self-esteem.
- **Work Environment:** A collaborative and inclusive work environment fosters personal growth by encouraging open communication, teamwork, and problem-solving. Conversely, a toxic or highly competitive culture can stifle growth and affect overall well-being.

5. Reasons for Resignation and Seeking Better Opportunities

Despite the structured environment and potential benefits of working in an MNC, several factors may lead an employee to resign and seek better opportunities:

- **Lack of Work-Life Balance:** Persistent long hours and inadequate work-life balance can lead to burnout and dissatisfaction. Employees may resign in search of roles that offer more flexibility and personal time.
- **Limited Career Growth:** If an employee feels that their career advancement opportunities are stagnant or that their contributions are not recognized, they might seek new positions that provide better growth prospects.
- **Work Culture Misalignment:** Discomfort with the company's culture, such as a lack of support, poor management practices, or a toxic work environment, can drive employees to look for workplaces that align better with their values and work style.
- **Desire for New Challenges:** Employees may leave to explore new fields or industries, seeking fresh challenges that align with their evolving career goals and personal interests.

- **Inadequate Compensation:** If compensation and benefits do not meet expectations or industry standards, employees might look for opportunities that offer better financial rewards and overall job satisfaction.

Conclusion

Navigating a career in a corporate office involves understanding the working style, performance review system, work-life balance, and the impact of work culture on personal development. While MNCs offer structured environments and professional growth opportunities, challenges such as work-life balance issues and work culture misalignments can lead employees to seek better opportunities. Addressing these factors thoughtfully can help employees make informed career decisions and find roles that align with their personal and professional goals.

CHAPTER TEN

From Orientation to Reality: A Deep Dive into Corporate Life at L&T

On the 1st of July 2019, an exhilarating yet daunting chapter of my professional journey began. The company, Larsen & Toubro (L&T), invited us for an orientation at a prestigious five-star hotel in Chennai, Tamil Nadu. This initiation was not merely a formality; it was a comprehensive 14 to 15-day training session combined with an orientation program, conducted at L&T's headquarters in Chennai. The sessions were scheduled from 9:00 AM to 5:00 PM on weekdays, promising an immersive experience into the corporate world.

Initially, everything about this orientation appeared to be splendid. The five-star accommodation was a luxury I had never encountered before. Each morning began with a lavish buffet breakfast, featuring an array of fruits, juices, and other healthy dishes that seemed like a dream come true. I had only seen such feasts in movies, where actors and actresses indulged in sumptuous spreads. It was surreal to experience this opulence firsthand.

Our mornings at the hotel were followed by a rush to the lecture halls at L&T's headquarters. We aimed to secure the best seats to avoid being called upon by lecturers for questions related to the presentations they delivered. These sessions were designed to provide us with an in-depth understanding of L&T's operations and culture. We meticulously gathered details about the company's workings, gradually familiarizing ourselves with its inner mechanics.

However, this phase of comfort was short-lived. On the 10th day, our accommodation was changed to a Tier-3 hotel—a three-star-rated establishment. This shift marked a notable departure from the luxurious hotel experience. From then on, transportation to the headquarters was arranged by L&T via cabs, replacing the earlier bus rides that had allowed us to bond and have fun with our colleagues. The camaraderie we had enjoyed during those bus rides was now a distant memory.

The final day of orientation arrived with a mix of anticipation and anxiety. It was the moment when the company would announce our postings. To my surprise, I was the only one assigned to the Pondicherry factory—a facility dedicated to manufacturing parts for Transmission Line Towers (TLT). While other sites at L&T were often dynamic and transient, this was a permanent, location-based job. At that moment, I was unaware of the formidable workload and challenges that awaited me in the days to come.

As an introvert, the prospect of working in a corporate environment filled me with trepidation. MNCs are notorious for their culture of regular, often intense, performance reviews. Managers frequently conduct periodic meetings to assess the progress of tasks assigned to subordinates, field staff, and workmen. These reviews typically involve presentations, either via PowerPoint slides or written directly on whiteboards, in front of a room full of colleagues. The pressure to provide satisfactory and convincing explanations to superiors can be overwhelming, especially when one's performance is scrutinized closely.

In the initial days at the factory, these intense evaluations were not immediately apparent. I was instructed to spend the first three months visiting the factory and learning the ropes. During this period, I occasionally attended presentation sessions and witnessed the corporate culture I had heard about. I was tasked with creating a PowerPoint presentation that outlined the skills I had acquired during training and proposed ideas for improving industrial operations in various departments.

Despite my efforts to complete the training successfully, I found myself increasingly preoccupied with thoughts of resignation. As I delved deeper into the realities of working at L&T, several unsettling observations came to light. I learned that employees who consistently received a rating of 4 in their appraisal reports for three consecutive years faced the risk of termination. I witnessed firsthand the harsh treatment of subordinates by managers, who often reacted angrily to failures. Staff members were frequently required to work late into the night, with the best performers expected to demonstrate exceptional dedication. The rigid schedule demanded early mornings, with employees required to catch a company-run bus and arrive at the office by 8:30 AM sharp. The job involved extensive follow-ups with multiple stakeholders across different departments, and fieldwork was a significant component. Tasks were ultimately dependent on the performance of workmen, with employees held accountable for the successful completion of these tasks. The limited number of staff members in each section led to overwhelming workloads, and the overall frustration was palpable.

These early insights into the job painted a grim picture, leading me to contemplate resignation. Yet, the financial responsibility towards my family made it difficult to abandon these thoughts. Despite my reservations, I resolved to continue for the time being and explore the possibility of preparing for the GATE entrance exam, with the goal of either pursuing higher studies or securing a position in a renowned PSU company. I informed my parents of my intentions, and they were mentally prepared for my decision to resign. However, a lack of courage prevented me from acting on my decision immediately. After six months of rigorous struggle and introspection, I decided to give the job a bit more time.

This decision marked the beginning of a challenging journey. I was assigned to the "Planning & Production Control" division, reputed to be one of the most demanding sections within the factory. As I delved into the responsibilities of this division, I quickly realized the gravity of my situation. The staff members were often abrasive, displaying a lack of patience in guiding me through the basics of daily tasks. Simple questions about processes were met with frustration and scorn. I was reprimanded for not knowing how to use Excel efficiently—a skill that, while not universally taught in college, was expected to be mastered. The constant reprimands and high expectations took a toll on my morale.

There were nights when I found myself in tears, overwhelmed by the difficulty of completing tasks and the fear of reprimand. Despite this, I dedicated myself to learning and gradually became more comfortable with the work. However, the daily progress meetings remained a source of anxiety. I often rushed to the office with a sense of dread, fearing that my performance would be scrutinized and criticized.

My health also began to suffer under the strain. The company's doctor regularly evaluated my blood pressure, which was consistently abnormal. He advised me to reduce my salt intake, unaware that my health issues were not merely a result of dietary choices. My manager, a South Indian, exhibited a clear bias against North Indian employees. His derisive remarks about my performance reflected an underlying prejudice. In L&T, the distinction between B.Tech holders and Diploma holders was stark. B.Tech graduates, or Graduate Engineer Trainees (GETs), were expected to deliver high standards of performance and were compensated accordingly. In contrast, Diploma holders, or Diploma Engineer Trainees (DETs), were held to different expectations. The term "Under-Performance" was often used to describe GETs who failed to meet these elevated standards, and it was a label I found myself struggling under.

The contrast between the glamorous orientation and the harsh realities of the job was stark. The initial allure of a five-star experience quickly gave way to the demanding and often unforgiving nature of corporate life at L&T. This experience was a profound learning curve, highlighting the challenges of working in a high-pressure environment and the complexities of adapting to a corporate culture that often felt at odds with personal values and expectations.

Reflecting on this journey, I realized that my time at L&T was not just about the professional challenges I faced but also about personal growth and self-discovery. The experience forced me to confront my fears, adapt to new environments, and navigate the intricate dynamics of corporate life. It underscored the importance of resilience, adaptability, and the need to make informed decisions about one's career path.

Ultimately, my time at L&T was a crucible that tested my limits and shaped my perspective on professional life. The lessons learned during this period, though challenging, were invaluable in understanding the realities of corporate work and in preparing for future endeavors. The journey from orientation to the realities of working at L&T was a transformative experience, one that provided insights into the complexities of the corporate world and the importance of aligning one's career choices with personal values and aspirations.

CHAPTER ELEVEN

Challenges and Realities of Working in L&T's PPC and Dispatch Departments

Challenges and Realities of Working in L&T's PPC and Dispatch Departments

Working in the Planning and Production Control (PPC) division of L&T was a multifaceted experience that involved a range of responsibilities and daily challenges. Here's a detailed look into the roles and tasks I handled during my tenure, as well as the hurdles and insights I gained.

Responsibilities in the PPC Division

1. **Planning of Raw Material:** My role required meticulous planning to ensure the optimal utilization of raw materials for the production of tower parts. I used a "machine-balancing" chart to manage the workflow efficiently. This chart was essentially a comprehensive table that included project names, details of the average monthly production capacity of machines, and the monthly load distributed among various machines based on project orders. The purpose was to determine if machines were under-loaded or overloaded, thus facilitating a balance

between production needs and machine capacity. This planning was crucial to minimizing idle time and maximizing production efficiency.

2. **Preparation of Material Cutting Sheet:** I was responsible for creating a material cutting sheet, a tool designed to optimize the use of raw materials. The aim was to minimize scrap and end-bits by accurately calculating the lengths required for different parts. By carefully planning cuts, we ensured that the scrap percentage remained within prescribed limits, which in turn helped in reducing waste and improving cost-efficiency.

3. **Preparing Raw Material Issue Slips:** Based on the cutting sheets, I prepared issue slips to facilitate the distribution of raw materials to various work centers from the steel yard. These slips were essential for managing inventory and ensuring that materials were available for production on CNC and manual machines. Coordination with the store-keeping in-charges was necessary to ensure accurate and timely issuance of materials.

4. **Following Up with Stakeholders:** My responsibilities included regular follow-ups with various stakeholders such as the Store In-charge, Production team, Fabrication and Galvanizing teams, and the Quality Control (QC) team. The goal was to minimize the rejection of finished goods at each stage and ensure that the final products met the required standards before being delivered to the dispatch team. This role required effective communication and coordination to ensure timely and satisfactory completion of tasks.

Transition to the Dispatch Department

After spending nearly two years in the PPC division, I was transferred to the Dispatch department. This transition marked a challenging phase in my career at L&T, characterized by a different set of responsibilities and difficulties.

1. **Adjustment to New Role:** The Dispatch department presented a stark contrast to my previous role. The work environment

was demanding, with a constant need to coordinate with truck drivers, crane operators, contractors, and various supervisors. This role required a blend of logistical management and interpersonal skills to handle the dispatch of goods efficiently.

2. **Challenges of Work-Life Balance:** During my time in Pondicherry, I faced significant lifestyle adjustments. The regional food habits were quite different from what I was accustomed to, and adapting to local cuisine proved challenging. Meals typically consisted of dosas, idlis, lemon rice, and other South Indian dishes, which were not always to my taste. In the evenings, options for food were limited, and I found myself frequently preparing simple meals or relying on local eateries with restricted choices.

3. **Living Conditions and Emotional Strain:** Living in a rented flat with two roommates, I often felt isolated and disconnected from my family and friends. My work schedule left little time for social interaction, and I struggled with feelings of loneliness and dissatisfaction. The lack of work-life balance and the demanding nature of the job contributed to a growing sense of frustration and anxiety about my career.

4. **Cultural and Language Barriers:** One of the significant challenges in the Dispatch department was dealing with cultural and language barriers. Being a Hindi speaker in a predominantly Tamil-speaking environment, I faced difficulties in communication and often felt excluded. The local supervisors and labor managers showed preference for Tamil-speaking staff, which created an environment of bias and favoritism. This exclusion, combined with the lack of support for my efforts, made it challenging to perform effectively.

5. **Internal Conflicts and Malpractices:** The work environment was marred by issues of internal conflicts and malpractices. The preference for local staff over Hindi-speaking employees led to a lack of cooperation and frequent disagreements. As an introvert and kind-hearted individual, I found it difficult to confront these issues openly, and the ongoing malpractices and favoritism

impacted my performance and morale.

Reflections and Decision to Resign

The combination of these challenges led me to a point where I had to reconsider my future at L&T. The pressures of the job, the cultural and language barriers, and the lack of work-life balance were significant factors in my decision-making process.

1. **Emotional and Mental Strain:** The emotional toll of working in an environment where I felt undervalued and unsupported was immense. The constant pressure to meet targets, coupled with the lack of personal satisfaction and the inability to enjoy my time off, contributed to a sense of despair and helplessness.

2. **Financial and Family Considerations:** During this period, my family faced financial difficulties, which further complicated my decision. I was hesitant to resign due to the potential impact on my family's financial situation, especially after recent personal events such as my grandfather's passing and my sister's marriage.

3. **Realization and Resignation:** After much contemplation and struggle, I realized that continuing in this environment was not conducive to my personal and professional growth. The lack of alignment between my values and the company's work culture, combined with the unsustainable work conditions, led me to make the difficult decision to resign. I began preparing for competitive exams, to explore opportunities for further studies or roles in organizations that offered a better work-life balance.

In conclusion, my experience at L&T was a complex and multifaceted journey. While it provided valuable insights into the corporate world and helped me develop certain skills, the challenges and difficulties I faced ultimately guided me toward seeking a career path that better aligns with my personal values and professional goals.

Key Takeaways from the story:

1. **Roles and Responsibilities in the PPC Division:**

   - **Raw Material Planning:** Involved optimizing machine usage and production capacity to minimize idle time and maximize efficiency.
   - **Material Cutting Sheet Preparation:** Focused on minimizing scrap by accurately planning material cuts.
   - **Issue Slip Preparation:** Ensured proper issuance of raw materials for production.
   - **Stakeholder Coordination:** Required managing communication between various teams to ensure timely and quality delivery of products.

2. **Challenges in the Dispatch Department:**

   - **Cultural and Language Barriers:** Encountered difficulties in communication and integration due to being a Hindi speaker in a Tamil-speaking environment.
   - **Work-Life Balance Issues:** Faced challenges adapting to local food habits and maintaining personal well-being due to demanding work hours.
   - **Living Conditions:** Experienced isolation and frustration due to limited social interaction and unsatisfactory living conditions.

3. **Emotional and Professional Strain:**

   - **Loneliness and Disconnection:** Felt isolated and disconnected from family and friends, impacting emotional well-being.
   - **Professional Challenges:** Encountered bias and favoritism, which affected performance and job satisfaction.

4. **Decision-Making and Resignation:**

- ◦ **Internal Conflicts and Malpractices:** Dealt with workplace issues such as favoritism and unethical practices.
- ◦ **Financial and Family Considerations:** Hesitated to resign due to financial implications and recent family events.
- ◦ **Career Realignment:** Decided to leave L&T and pursue further studies or seek opportunities in organizations with a better work-life balance.

5. **Personal Growth and Reflection:**

- ◦ **Self-Awareness:** Recognized the mismatch between personal values and the corporate culture at L&T.
- ◦ **Career Path Reevaluation:** Used the experience to reassess career goals and explore new opportunities aligned with personal values and career aspirations.

Overall, the story highlights the complexities and challenges of working in a high-pressure corporate environment, particularly in roles that involve significant responsibilities and require adaptation to a new work culture. It underscores the importance of aligning career choices with personal values and well-being.

The story conveys several key messages about the challenges and realities of working in a high-pressure corporate environment, especially in roles that involve significant responsibilities and require adaptation to new work cultures:

1. **Understanding the Role and Responsibilities:**

- ◦ **Complexity of Duties:** Corporate roles, such as those in Planning & Production Control (PPC) and Dispatch departments, involve intricate responsibilities, including material planning, production optimization, and coordination across multiple teams. Understanding and managing these responsibilities are crucial for effective job performance.

2. **Challenges of Corporate Life:**

   ◦ **Cultural and Language Barriers:** Adapting to a new work environment can be challenging, especially when there are cultural and language differences. These barriers can impact communication, integration, and overall job satisfaction.
   ◦ **Work-Life Balance:** Corporate jobs often come with demanding schedules and expectations, which can affect personal well-being and work-life balance. This is particularly true when adapting to new living conditions and local customs.

3. **Emotional and Professional Strain:**

   ◦ **Isolation and Loneliness:** The experience of working in a new location can lead to feelings of isolation and loneliness, impacting mental and emotional health.
   ◦ **Professional Challenges:** Facing bias, favoritism, and unethical practices can undermine job satisfaction and professional growth. These challenges can be exacerbated by personal traits, such as being introverted or kind-hearted, which may not align with the corporate culture.

4. **Decision-Making and Career Management:**

   ◦ **Evaluating Fit:** It is important to evaluate whether a job and its environment align with personal values and career goals. The mismatch between personal values and corporate culture can lead to dissatisfaction and a need for career realignment.
   ◦ **Resignation and Career Shifts:** Deciding to leave a job can be difficult, especially when considering financial implications and family concerns. However, sometimes it is necessary to prioritize personal well-being and seek opportunities that better align with one's values and career aspirations.

5. **Personal Growth and Reflection:**

  - **Self-Awareness:** Gaining a deeper understanding of one's strengths, weaknesses, and career preferences is crucial for making informed decisions about career paths.
  - **Career Realignment:** Using experiences to reassess and realign career goals can lead to more fulfilling and sustainable career choices.

Overall, the passage highlights the importance of aligning career choices with personal values, the challenges of adapting to new work environments, and the need for resilience and self-awareness in navigating corporate careers.

The passage reveals a range of complex and deeply personal feelings experienced by the author throughout their journey with L&T. These feelings include:

1. **Initial Excitement and Subsequent Disillusionment:**

  - **Excitement:** The author initially felt excitement and a sense of achievement when starting the orientation and training at L&T, particularly enjoying the perks like staying in a five-star hotel and experiencing new aspects of corporate life.
  - **Disillusionment:** This excitement soon gave way to disillusionment as the reality of the job and its challenges set in, leading to feelings of frustration and uncertainty about their future.

2. **Isolation and Loneliness:**

  - **Loneliness:** The author describes a profound sense of isolation while living in a new location, struggling with unfamiliar food and a lack of social interaction. This loneliness was exacerbated by the demanding work schedule and the distance from family and familiar support networks.

3. **Frustration and Stress:**

    ◦ **Work Pressure:** The author experienced significant stress from the demanding nature of the job, including the pressure to meet high standards, handle difficult responsibilities, and manage interpersonal conflicts in the workplace.
    ◦ **Emotional Strain:** The constant pressure, long hours, and challenging work environment led to emotional strain, including anxiety and a sense of inadequacy. The author struggled with physical symptoms of stress, such as abnormal blood pressure readings.

4. **Conflict and Self-Doubt:**

    ◦ **Cultural and Language Barriers:** The author felt frustrated and marginalized due to cultural and language barriers, which contributed to self-doubt and a sense of exclusion within the workplace.
    ◦ **Self-Doubt:** The author grappled with self-doubt, questioning their ability to succeed in the corporate environment and feeling overwhelmed by the mismatch between their personal traits and the company culture.

5. **Decision-Making Struggles:**

    ◦ **Resignation Dilemma:** The author faced an internal conflict about resigning from the job, torn between the desire for a more balanced and fulfilling career and the financial responsibilities and family expectations that made the decision difficult.
    ◦ **Regret and Reflection:** There is a sense of regret about not making the decision to resign earlier, coupled with reflection on the lessons learned and the need for personal growth and career reassessment.

6. **Empowerment and Determination:**

   ◦ **Determination:** Despite the challenges, the author demonstrated determination to improve their situation, learn new skills, and navigate the difficulties of the job. This determination reflects a drive to overcome obstacles and seek a better alignment with their career goals.

7. **Longing for Better Work-Life Balance:**

   ◦ **Desire for Balance:** The author expresses a strong desire for a better work-life balance, recognizing that the demanding nature of the job at L&T was incompatible with their personal needs and well-being.

In summary, the author's feelings throughout the passage encompass a broad spectrum of emotions, including initial enthusiasm, growing frustration, loneliness, self-doubt, and a desire for a more fulfilling and balanced career. These emotions reflect the challenges and personal growth experienced during their time at L&T.

CHAPTER TWELVE

Insights of Despatch Department

The Challenges and Lessons of Working in the Dispatch Department

In the life of any professional, there are moments that define the trajectory of their career and personal well-being. My tenure in the Dispatch Department was one such defining period. As a Mechanical Engineer with a background from NIT Manipur and experience as a Senior Engineer at L&T Construction, I had anticipated a challenging yet rewarding career. However, my stint at the Dispatch Department exposed me to trials that tested my limits and reshaped my perspective on work and life. This narrative details the multifaceted challenges I encountered, the lessons I learned, and the critical decision I ultimately made regarding my career.

Understanding the Department's Workflow

To grasp the intricacies of my role, it's essential to first understand the sequence of tasks expected within the Dispatch Department. This sequence outlines how various responsibilities interlink and build upon each other, setting the stage for the complexities that arise in daily operations.

1. **Follow-ups with the Production Team:** The Dispatch Department plays a crucial role in ensuring that TLT parts, which are galvanized for durability, reach their designated sites.

These parts are produced through a two-stage process. Initially, raw materials are fabricated into the required shapes and sizes using either CNC machines or manual machinery. The second stage involves galvanization, where the fabricated parts are coated with zinc for increased longevity.

Once the parts are ready, the Dispatch Department's responsibility is to manage the "panel-packing" process. This involves organizing and preparing these parts for dispatch, ensuring that they are ready for transportation to the construction sites.

1. **Panel-Packing Process:** The panel-packing process represents one of the most challenging aspects of the dispatch department and, indeed, the entire factory operation. This process is pivotal in ensuring that all parts are properly prepared and dispatched for the assembly of TL (Transmission Line) towers. The complexity and scale of this task necessitate a detailed examination to understand its intricacies and the challenges involved.

- **I. Storage and Retrieval of Parts**

Storage Conditions: Parts arriving from the galvanizing department are typically stored in a chaotic manner, spread across a vast area of 2-3 kilometers. This disorganized storage makes it exceedingly difficult to locate specific items when needed. Parts are often piled haphazardly, creating a daunting task for those responsible for retrieving them.

Movement and Handling: To manage this disarray, mobile cranes and gantry cranes are employed to move parts from their storage locations to the designated areas for panel-packing. The sheer volume and weight of these parts necessitate the use of heavy machinery to facilitate their movement and prevent damage.

- **II. The Panel-Packing Process**

Understanding Panels: A panel is a crucial component of a TL tower, which is constructed in segments for efficiency. The panels include various parts such as the legs, the body, and the cross-arms of the tower. Each panel has specific requirements regarding the parts it must contain, and these requirements are detailed in a comprehensive list.

Identification and Bundling: Each part, whether small, medium, or heavy, is embossed with a part name. The panel-packing process involves locating each part from the disorganized heaps and assembling them into bundles according to the specifications outlined for each panel. The process is not complete until every part on the list is found and bundled correctly.

- **III. Challenges in the Panel-Packing Process**

Difficulty in Finding Parts: The challenge of locating specific parts amidst the heaps is particularly acute for smaller components. These small parts can be easily overlooked or buried under larger items, making retrieval a strenuous and time-consuming task.

Time Constraints and Penalties: The urgency of meeting project deadlines adds to the pressure. If parts are not ready on time, the company may face significant penalties due to delays. Containers or trucks waiting for dispatch can exacerbate the situation, leading to financial repercussions if the packing process is incomplete.

Physical Strain: The search for parts often involves working in harsh conditions, such as extreme heat, which can lead to physical exhaustion. Employees may find themselves sweating profusely and working long hours, including night shifts, to meet deadlines.

Handling Heavy Parts: Heavy parts, especially those for the tower legs, pose additional challenges. These parts are sometimes located under even heavier items, making them difficult to access. Moving these heavy components requires cranes, which may not always be readily available due to competing demands.

Resource Allocation Issues: The allocation of cranes and other resources can lead to conflicts among staff members. When resources are scarce, the question of which task is more urgent becomes a point of contention. This can create a competitive environment where employees are forced to "fight" for access to necessary equipment.

Workplace Dynamics: The disparity in how staff members are treated based on their regional backgrounds can further complicate the process. For instance, local workers may receive preferential treatment over those from other regions, leading to uneven communication and cooperation.

- **IV. Strategies to Overcome Challenges**

Enhanced Storage Solutions: To mitigate disorganization, it's essential to implement a systematic approach to storage. This includes clearly labeling parts and organizing storage areas to facilitate easier retrieval.

Improved Inventory Management: Adopting advanced inventory management systems can significantly streamline the panel-packing process. These systems help track part locations and reduce the time spent searching for components.

Efficient Resource Management: Develop a well-defined plan for resource allocation, including cranes and trucks. Utilize scheduling tools to manage resource availability and ensure that the most urgent tasks receive priority.

Physical Support and Ergonomics: Provide employees with training on safe lifting techniques and invest in ergonomic tools to reduce physical strain. Regular breaks and health programs can help manage the physical demands of the job.

Clear Communication Channels: Establish clear communication channels to address resource allocation disputes and ensure that all team members are informed about project priorities and deadlines.

Fair Treatment and Inclusivity: Promote a culture of fairness and inclusivity within the workplace. Ensure that all staff members are treated equally, regardless of their regional backgrounds, and foster a collaborative environment.

Stress Management: Implement stress management programs to support employees dealing with high-pressure situations. Offer access to counseling and support services to help manage workplace stress and prevent burnout.

By addressing these challenges with targeted strategies, the panel-packing process can be optimized for greater efficiency and effectiveness. Ensuring that each step is well-managed and that employees are supported will contribute to smoother operations and better overall outcomes.

1. **Ensuring Dispatch of Packed Parts:** Once the panel-packing process is complete, the packed parts must be loaded onto containers for international projects or trucks for domestic projects. Supervisors are responsible for maintaining a list of loaded parts, which is later updated in Excel sheets to track the project's progress.

   The accuracy of this documentation is vital for ensuring that the correct parts reach the intended destinations. It also helps in managing the overall project timeline and addressing any discrepancies that may arise during transportation.

4. **Management Tasks:** Effective management is a key component of the Dispatch Department's operations. Responsibilities include overseeing workmen and contractors, coordinating with crane operators, ensuring timely delivery of raw materials, and working closely with the production team to expedite the completion of parts.

   Managing these aspects requires a high level of organization and communication skills. It also involves addressing any issues that arise promptly and ensuring that all tasks are completed in accordance with project priorities.

Daily Roles and Responsibilities

The daily roles and responsibilities within the Dispatch Department are varied and demanding. Each day presents a new set of challenges that require careful attention and proactive management.

1. **Analysis of Pending Dispatch Details:** At the start of each day, it is crucial to analyze the pending dispatch details for ongoing projects. This involves reviewing the progress of each project, identifying any delays, and conducting meetings to address these issues. Regular analysis helps in maintaining an overview of the project's status and ensures that any potential problems are addressed in a timely manner.

2. **Field Work:** Fieldwork involves physically inspecting the storage areas to identify and retrieve pending parts. This task requires a detailed understanding of the parts and their locations, as well as the ability to coordinate effectively with workmen. It often involves printing reports, listing pending items, and assigning tasks to workmen for part identification.

3. **Crane Allocation:** Cranes are essential for the movement of parts within the factory. Identifying available cranes and coordinating with drivers is a key responsibility. This task requires an understanding of the project's priorities and ensuring that cranes are allocated based on the urgency of the tasks.

4. **Setting Packing Priorities:** Instructing contractors and workmen on packing priorities is crucial for meeting project deadlines. This involves directing efforts towards the most urgent projects and ensuring that panels are packed and dispatched in the correct order.

5. **Vehicle Requirements:** Planning for vehicle placement involves assessing the size of the panels and the status of packed panels. Coordination with the logistics team is necessary to ensure that

the appropriate vehicles are available and ready for loading.

6. **Ensuring Timely Loading:** Ensuring that vehicles are loaded on time is vital to avoid delays. This involves overseeing the loading process and ensuring that vehicles do not exceed the free loading time, which could result in additional costs.

7. **Sending Intimations to Site Staff:** Communicating with site staff about the delivery status is essential for coordinating the arrival of parts and ensuring that construction timelines are met. This involves sending dispatch reports and providing updates on delivery schedules.

8. **Miscellaneous Works:** Miscellaneous tasks include addressing shortages, managing manpower, and ensuring proper storage of parts. It also involves coordinating with the production team for reproducing shortage items and assisting workmen in locating parts for urgent dispatch.

The Challenges of Working in the Dispatch Department

Working in the Dispatch Department presented several significant challenges, each contributing to a demanding and high-pressure environment.

1. **Handling Disorganized Heaps:** The disorganized storage of parts posed a major challenge. Parts often arrived in untidy heaps, making it difficult to locate specific items. This disorganization required intensive manual searching and coordination with workmen, often under challenging conditions.

2. **Physical Demands:** The physical demands of the job were considerable. Working in harsh weather conditions, lifting heavy parts, and operating cranes required physical stamina and resilience. The demanding nature of the work often led to exhaustion and physical strain.

3. **Pressure to Meet Deadlines:** Meeting project deadlines was a constant pressure. Delays in dispatching parts could result in penalties and impact project timelines. This pressure was

exacerbated by the need to work long hours and sometimes through the night to complete urgent tasks.

4. **Managing Resources:** Coordinating the availability of cranes, vehicles, and workmen required effective resource management. The challenge was to balance competing demands and ensure that resources were allocated efficiently to meet project requirements.

5. **Dealing with Errors and Shortages:** Errors in part identification or shortages could have significant consequences. Addressing these issues required prompt action and coordination with the production team to avoid delays and financial losses.

6. **Workplace Dynamics:** Navigating workplace dynamics and managing relationships with colleagues and superiors was another challenge. Conflicts over resource allocation and differing priorities could create tension and impact team cohesion.

Personal Struggles and Lessons Learned

My experience in the Dispatch Department was marked by personal struggles that tested my limits and led to valuable lessons.

1. **Experiencing High Pressure:** The high-pressure environment took a toll on my mental and physical health. The constant stress, coupled with long hours and demanding tasks, led to feelings of anxiety and depression. The realization that this pressure was unsustainable prompted me to reassess my situation.

2. **Dealing with Criticism:** Facing criticism from managers and superiors was a recurring issue. The negative feedback, particularly when tasks were not completed as expected, created a sense of frustration and helplessness. This criticism often felt unjust, especially when efforts were made to meet demanding deadlines.

3. **Making Sacrifices:** The need to work long hours, including night shifts, resulted in significant sacrifices. Personal time and well-

being were compromised, and the constant demand to meet deadlines took precedence over other aspects of life. This sacrifice led to a reconsideration of priorities and the importance of work-life balance.

4. **The Decision to Resign:** The culmination of these struggles led me to make the difficult decision to resign. The final straw was an incident involving the mismanagement of shortage items. Despite my best efforts to verify the information, a mistake was made, leading to severe criticism from my manager. This incident, combined with ongoing stress and dissatisfaction, made me realize that resigning was the best option for my well-being.

5. **The Importance of Self-Preservation:** The experience underscored the importance of self-preservation and the need to prioritize personal health and happiness. No job is worth sacrificing one's well-being, and making tough decisions for oneself is crucial for long-term success and satisfaction.

Advice to Readers

To those facing similar challenges, my advice is straightforward:

1. **Prioritize Your Well-Being:** Your health and well-being are paramount. If a job is causing undue stress and affecting your health, it is important to reassess your situation and consider making changes.

2. **Be Prepared to Make Tough Decisions:** Making difficult decisions, such as resigning from a job, can be challenging but necessary for your overall well-being. Don't hesitate to take action if it means improving your quality of life.

3. **Seek Support:** Seek support from your seniors and parents to take decisions for yourselves.

Major challenges described in the above passage:
1. **Disorganized Storage of Parts**
Description:

- Parts often arrived in large, disorganized heaps spread over 2-3 kilometers. This disorganization made it difficult to find specific parts quickly, leading to inefficiencies in the packing process.

Impact:

- Time-consuming manual searches were necessary to locate parts.
- Increased risk of errors in identifying and bundling parts, potentially delaying dispatch.
- Physical strain on employees due to extensive searching and handling of parts.

2. Physical Demands of the Job
Description:

- The role required substantial physical effort, including lifting heavy parts, working in harsh weather conditions, and operating cranes.

Impact:

- Risk of physical injury or long-term health issues from handling heavy parts and operating machinery.
- Exhaustion from prolonged physical activity and working long hours.
- Challenges in maintaining productivity and accuracy under physical strain.

3. Pressure to Meet Deadlines
Description:

- The Dispatch Department faced significant pressure to meet strict project deadlines, with potential penalties for delays. This often involved working long hours and sometimes overnight shifts to complete tasks on time.

Impact:

- Increased stress and anxiety due to the constant pressure to perform.
- Reduced work-life balance, leading to burnout and decreased job satisfaction.
- Potential for mistakes and oversights due to fatigue from extended working hours.

4. Resource Management
Description:

- Managing the allocation of cranes, vehicles, and workmen was a complex task, requiring efficient coordination to meet project demands.

Impact:

- Difficulty in balancing competing demands for limited resources, potentially leading to delays.
- Increased pressure to prioritize tasks and manage resource availability effectively.
- Conflicts and competition among staff for access to critical resources like cranes.

5. Errors and Shortages
Description:

- Errors in identifying or managing parts, particularly shortages or lost items, could have significant financial and operational consequences.

Impact:

- Financial losses due to the need to reproduce lost or incorrect parts.
- Potential delays in project completion, impacting client satisfaction and contractual obligations.
- Increased pressure on staff to correct errors and manage shortages promptly.

6. Workplace Dynamics and Conflicts
Description:

- Navigating workplace dynamics, including conflicts over resource allocation and differing priorities, created tension among team members and superiors.

Impact:

- Reduced team cohesion and morale due to interpersonal conflicts and competition.
- Challenges in maintaining effective communication and collaboration with colleagues and supervisors.
- Increased stress from managing conflicts and aligning with differing priorities.

7. High Pressure and Stress
Description:

- The high-pressure environment led to significant stress and anxiety, impacting both mental and physical health.

Impact:

- Increased risk of mental health issues such as anxiety and depression.
- Physical symptoms of stress, such as fatigue and impaired immune function.

- Reduced overall job satisfaction and well-being.

8. Criticism from Managers
Description:

- Facing frequent criticism and negative feedback from managers, especially when tasks were not completed as expected, created feelings of frustration and helplessness.

Impact:

- Decreased self-esteem and motivation due to constant negative feedback.
- Potential for increased stress and anxiety from fear of further criticism.
- Impact on job performance and overall morale due to perceived unfair treatment.

9. Sacrifices and Work-Life Balance
Description:

- The demanding nature of the job resulted in personal sacrifices and a compromised work-life balance, affecting overall well-being.

Impact:

- Strained personal relationships and reduced time for leisure activities.
- Increased risk of burnout and dissatisfaction due to lack of personal time and relaxation.
- Difficulty in maintaining a healthy work-life balance, leading to long-term negative effects on health and happiness.

10. Decision-Making Under Pressure

Description:

- Making tough decisions, such as resigning due to overwhelming stress and criticism, was a significant challenge.

Impact:

- Emotional and psychological strain from making life-altering decisions under pressure.
- Uncertainty about the future and potential career consequences of resignation.
- The need to balance personal well-being with professional responsibilities.

11. Managing Lost or Shortage Items
Description:

- Identifying and managing lost or shortage items, particularly heavy ones, was challenging and could result in financial losses if not managed correctly.

Impact:

- Increased complexity and difficulty in locating and handling heavy or small parts.
- Financial implications of reproducing lost parts and potential delays in project timelines.
- Additional stress from the pressure to resolve shortages promptly and accurately.

12. Communication and Coordination
Description:

- Effective communication and coordination with workmen, supervisors, and logistics teams were crucial but challenging due to the complexity and urgency of tasks.

Impact:

- Difficulty in ensuring that all parties are aligned and informed about project status and priorities.
- Increased risk of miscommunication and misunderstandings, leading to errors and delays.
- Pressure to maintain clear and effective communication channels in a high-stress environment.

These challenges illustrate the demanding nature of the Dispatch Department role and the various obstacles that can affect job performance and personal well-being. Addressing these challenges requires resilience, effective management strategies, and a focus on maintaining both professional and personal balance.

Message

Navigating the challenges faced in the Dispatch Department requires a deep understanding of the demanding nature of the role and the impact it has on both personal and professional life. The experiences described reveal significant stressors, from physical demands to high-pressure deadlines, and the need for effective management and coordination. It's crucial to acknowledge these challenges, seek appropriate solutions, and maintain a balance that supports overall well-being.

Solutions to Challenges

1. Disorganized Storage of Parts

Solution:

- **Implement Systematic Storage:** Develop and enforce a systematic approach to storing parts, including clear labeling and organized storage areas to reduce disorganization.
- **Use Technology:** Invest in inventory management software that helps track parts and their locations, making retrieval more efficient.

- **Regular Audits:** Conduct regular audits to ensure that parts are stored correctly and address any issues of disorganization promptly.

2. Physical Demands of the Job
Solution:

- **Provide Adequate Training:** Train staff on proper lifting techniques and safe handling procedures to minimize physical strain and prevent injuries.
- **Improve Ergonomics:** Invest in ergonomic equipment and tools that reduce physical strain, such as mechanical lifting aids and supportive footwear.
- **Offer Health Programs:** Implement health and wellness programs that include physical fitness and stress management to help employees cope with physical demands.

3. Pressure to Meet Deadlines
Solution:

- **Prioritize Tasks:** Use project management tools to prioritize tasks and manage deadlines effectively. Breaking down tasks into smaller, manageable steps can help reduce pressure.
- **Set Realistic Goals:** Work with management to set realistic deadlines based on current capabilities and resource availability.
- **Encourage Open Communication:** Foster open communication with supervisors about workload and deadlines to manage expectations and negotiate more achievable timelines.

4. Resource Management
Solution:

- **Develop a Resource Allocation Plan:** Create a comprehensive resource management plan that includes clear guidelines for the allocation of cranes, vehicles, and workmen.

- **Implement Scheduling Systems:** Use scheduling systems to track the availability of resources and ensure they are allocated efficiently based on project needs.
- **Foster Collaboration:** Promote a collaborative environment where team members can share resources and coordinate efforts to meet project demands.

5. Errors and Shortages
Solution:

- **Implement Quality Control Procedures:** Establish quality control procedures to minimize errors in part identification and management.
- **Track and Analyze Errors:** Keep detailed records of errors and shortages to identify patterns and address underlying issues.
- **Develop Contingency Plans:** Create contingency plans for managing shortages and reproducing parts to minimize disruptions and financial losses.

6. Workplace Dynamics and Conflicts
Solution:

- **Promote Team Building:** Invest in team-building activities and workshops to improve collaboration and resolve conflicts.
- **Provide Conflict Resolution Training:** Offer training on conflict resolution and effective communication to help staff navigate workplace dynamics.
- **Encourage Feedback:** Foster a culture of open feedback where employees can address issues constructively and work together to find solutions.

7. High Pressure and Stress
Solution:

- **Implement Stress Management Programs:** Introduce stress management programs that include techniques for relaxation, mindfulness, and work-life balance.
- **Provide Support Resources:** Offer access to mental health resources, such as counseling services and employee assistance programs (EAPs).
- **Encourage Regular Breaks:** Promote the importance of regular breaks and downtime to prevent burnout and maintain overall well-being.

8. Criticism from Managers
Solution:

- **Provide Constructive Feedback:** Encourage managers to offer constructive feedback that focuses on development and improvement rather than criticism.
- **Seek Regular Check-Ins:** Schedule regular check-ins with managers to discuss progress, address concerns, and receive guidance.
- **Develop Resilience:** Work on building resilience and coping strategies to handle criticism constructively and maintain confidence.

9. Sacrifices and Work-Life Balance
Solution:

- **Encourage Work-Life Balance:** Promote policies and practices that support a healthy work-life balance, such as flexible working hours and remote work options.
- **Set Boundaries:** Establish clear boundaries between work and personal life to prevent work from encroaching on personal time.
- **Encourage Time Off:** Encourage employees to take regular time off and use vacation days to recharge and maintain well-being.

10. Decision-Making Under Pressure
Solution:

- **Provide Decision-Making Support:** Offer support and resources to help employees make informed decisions under pressure, including access to mentors and decision-making frameworks.
- **Foster a Supportive Environment:** Create a supportive environment where employees feel comfortable seeking help and discussing difficult decisions.
- **Evaluate Options:** Encourage a thorough evaluation of options and potential outcomes to make well-informed decisions.

11. Managing Lost or Shortage Items
Solution:

- **Enhance Tracking Systems:** Improve tracking systems to reduce the incidence of lost or misplaced items, including better labeling and inventory management.
- **Improve Retrieval Processes:** Develop more efficient retrieval processes for managing shortages and ensuring timely reproduction of parts.
- **Increase Accountability:** Assign clear responsibility for managing lost or shortage items to ensure prompt resolution and reduce the risk of financial losses.

12. Communication and Coordination
Solution:

- **Enhance Communication Channels:** Implement effective communication channels and tools to ensure clear and timely information sharing among team members.
- **Regular Meetings:** Hold regular meetings to discuss project status, address issues, and coordinate efforts among different teams.

- **Improve Coordination Procedures:** Develop and enforce procedures for coordinating tasks and resources to ensure smooth operations and avoid misunderstandings.

By addressing these challenges with targeted solutions, employees and organizations can improve operational efficiency, enhance job satisfaction, and maintain a healthy work environment

CHAPTER THIRTEEN

Navigating Resignation and the Notice Period Transition

Resignation Decision and Notice Period

Despite considerable persuasion from my manager and senior leadership to reconsider my decision to resign, I stood firm and submitted my resignation letter. My superiors, deeply invested in retaining their staff, made every effort to convince me to stay, but I was resolute in my decision. After a few days, my resignation was officially accepted, marking the beginning of my notice period.

The notice period was not merely a formality but rather the starting point of a significant transition in my life. This phase signified the shift from a stable employment scenario to an uncertain period of unemployment, followed by a rigorous preparation journey for competitive exams. My focus shifted entirely from my professional responsibilities to preparing for a new career path in the banking sector.

Preparation for Banking Exams

The transition involved a deep dive into the syllabus for banking exams. I began by researching and understanding the various aspects of these exams, including the types of questions, the exam patterns, and the general pressure associated with them. To gain a better grasp of what to expect, I applied for several positions in the banking sector through the IBPS (Institute of Banking Personnel Selection) website. This initial step was crucial in understanding the level of questions and the overall exam environment.

Recognizing the need for structured learning, I turned to free online resources to build a solid foundation. YouTube became a valuable tool in this endeavor. I focused on two primary areas: reasoning and quantitative aptitude. For reasoning, I found Bankers Adda, which featured lectures by Saurav Singh Sir. For quantitative aptitude, I turned to Career Definer, where **Kaushik Mohanty Sir** offered detailed and engaging lessons.

Kaushik Mohanty Sir, in particular, earned my admiration for his exceptional teaching methods in quantitative subjects. His lectures were thorough and insightful, making complex concepts more accessible. I dedicated significant time to completing all available lectures from Career Definer, appreciating the clarity and depth of his instruction. I learned, from his excellent skills of solving Data intrepretation problems in a very less time and his knowledge in solving arithmetic problems is fabulous. He literally helped me in excel my knowledge in this part of preparation.

Study Strategies and Challenges

To optimize my study time, I opted for night shifts. This choice allowed me to study uninterrupted during the night, freeing me from the routine tasks and distractions of the daytime. During these night shifts, I focused intensely on my studies, particularly on quantitative aptitude. Over the course of three months, I managed to complete the entire syllabus for this subject using the free resources available online.

However, this approach took a toll on my health. The shift to nocturnal studying resulted in significant weight loss and the development of dark circles under my eyes. My health deteriorated progressively as I prioritized my preparation over my well-being.

In the workplace, this shift in focus led to complications. My managers continued to assign me tasks with the expectation that they would be completed on time. I frequently fell short of these expectations, only giving assurances without meeting deadlines.

This lack of productivity led to criticism from my managers, who questioned my future potential and capability. The work culture at L&T, which emphasized long hours over efficiency, added to my dissatisfaction.

Corporate Culture and Resignation

The corporate environment at L&T was characterized by a relentless focus on long hours and constant pressure to meet deadlines. While the company publicly espoused the importance of work-life balance, the reality was quite different. Employees were often expected to work late into the night, and failure to meet deadlines could result in severe consequences, including negative performance reviews and threats of termination.

This disconnect between the company's stated values and its actual practices contributed to my decision to resign. The pressure to continuously work long hours, coupled with the lack of recognition and appropriate rewards for the efforts of employees, made it clear that staying at L&T was no longer viable for me. I felt that my decision to resign was a necessary step towards a healthier and more fulfilling career path.

New Opportunities and Reflections

After submitting my resignation, I embarked on a new phase of preparation for competitive exams. During my notice period, I applied for the IBPS Clerk exam, with the preliminary exam scheduled for December 20, 2021. Although I was not fully prepared by that time, I concentrated on the essential topics for the prelims. I covered the basic syllabus for reasoning using YouTube sessions from Ankush Lamba Sir, focusing specifically on the topics relevant to the preliminary exam.

On the day of the exam, I managed to solve 79 out of 100 questions in my shift. The feedback from my performance in the preliminary exam was encouraging. Despite not being fully prepared for the mains, I felt positive about my progress and determined to continue my preparation.

I also took the SBI PO (State Bank of India Probationary Officer) exam but did not make it past the selection process. Nevertheless, scoring 50 out of 100 and coming close to the cutoff was a confidence booster. It reaffirmed my belief that with more focused preparation, I could achieve my goals.

My success in the IBPS Clerk prelims was a significant milestone. I was selected for the mains exam, scheduled for January 25, 2022. Although I was aware that I was not fully prepared for the mains, I used this opportunity to further refine my study techniques and approach.

Despite my best efforts, I was not selected in the final list for the IBPS Clerk exam, missing the cutoff by six marks. While this outcome was disappointing, I took it as a learning experience. I recognized that the journey was far from over and that further preparation and perseverance would be necessary to achieve my goals.

Conclusion

Reflecting on my transition from employment to competitive exam preparation, I believe that resigning from L&T was a pivotal decision in my life. It allowed me to focus on a new career path and take control of my professional destiny. The challenges and experiences I faced during this period have shaped my approach to career development and personal growth.

To anyone considering a similar transition, my advice is to remain steadfast in pursuing your goals and to not be discouraged by setbacks. The journey may be difficult, but it is through these challenges that we grow and find new opportunities. Embrace the journey with determination and focus, and remember that perseverance and hard work can lead to success.

Shift in Focus: Maruti Suzuki Exam and Its Consequences
Unexpected Opportunity and Its Impact

As I navigated through my notice period at L&T, a significant and unexpected opportunity emerged: I was invited to participate in the entrance exam for Maruti Suzuki. This came at a pivotal moment in my career transition, where I was deeply engrossed in preparing for banking exams. The chance to interview for a position at Maruti Suzuki, known for its attractive compensation packages, seemed like a promising detour from my planned path.

The interview was scheduled for October 18, 2021. This date was crucial, falling within the final month of my tenure at L&T, which was set to end on November 18, 2021. The Maruti Suzuki interview was to be conducted in Haryana, a journey that required substantial planning and travel. I arrived at a prestigious four-star hotel where the interview was held. The experience was a mix of excitement and anxiety. The luxurious setting and the professional demeanor of the interviewers added to the gravity of the situation, making it a memorable event in my career journey.

Upon completing the interview, I returned to my residence in Pondicherry. The prospect of a lucrative offer from Maruti Suzuki had a profound impact on my focus and priorities. The compensation package offered by Maruti Suzuki was highly appealing and caused me to reassess my current trajectory. As a result, I found myself increasingly distracted from my primary goal of preparing for competitive banking exams.

Distraction from Preparation

The allure of the Maruti Suzuki opportunity led me to shift my focus significantly. Instead of dedicating my final month at L&T to rigorous exam preparation, I became preoccupied with the anticipation of receiving a decision from Maruti Suzuki. This preoccupation was not merely a fleeting distraction; it consumed my time and energy. I found myself obsessively checking my email for any updates regarding the selection status, even at late hours, around 2 a.m. My nights became filled with anxiety and restless anticipation as I awaited news.

This shift in focus had a detrimental effect on my preparation. The final month of my notice period, which was originally intended for intensive study, was instead consumed by this distraction. I had initially planned to use this time to deepen my understanding of key concepts and practice extensively, but my fixation on the Maruti Suzuki outcome led to wasted opportunities. My preparation for competitive exams stagnated, leaving me in a position where I felt like a novice, despite having invested several months in study and preparation.

Consequences of the Distraction

By the time my notice period concluded on November 18, 2021, I was acutely aware of the consequences of my distraction. I had failed to make substantial progress in my competitive exam preparation. The final month, which should have been a period of consolidation and refinement of my skills, had been marred by my preoccupation with the Maruti Suzuki opportunity.

On November 27, 2021, I packed my belongings and prepared to return home. This marked the end of my tenure at L&T and the beginning of a new chapter in my career. As I left Pondicherry, I faced the reality that I had to refocus on my original goal of preparing for competitive exams. The experience with Maruti Suzuki, while valuable in its own right, had inadvertently led me to lose precious time and momentum in my exam preparation.

Refocusing and Moving Forward

Returning home marked a significant turning point. Despite the distraction caused by the Maruti Suzuki interview, I was determined to restart my preparation with renewed vigor. The allure of the Maruti Suzuki opportunity had faded, and I was now more focused on the task at hand: preparing for competitive exams.

The transition from L&T to my home environment presented its own set of challenges. The shift from corporate life to intensive exam preparation required a reassessment of my strategy and approach. I needed to make up for lost time and regain the momentum I had lost. The challenge was not just about picking up where I left off but also about ensuring that I approached my preparation with a fresh perspective and renewed energy.

Reflecting on the Journey

Reflecting on this period of transition, I recognized that while the Maruti Suzuki opportunity was a significant and appealing diversion, it ultimately taught me valuable lessons. The experience highlighted the importance of maintaining focus on long-term goals and not allowing temporary distractions to derail well-laid plans. The competitive exam preparation journey was not just about acquiring knowledge but also about managing distractions and staying committed to one's objectives.

In summary, the period following my resignation from L&T was marked by a significant distraction due to the Maruti Suzuki opportunity. This diversion, while initially promising, ultimately led to a loss of valuable preparation time. However, as I moved forward, I was able to refocus on my competitive exam preparation with a clearer understanding of my priorities and a renewed commitment to achieving my goals.

Transitioning from Employment to Exam Preparation: A Detailed Journey

The Courage to Resign and the Challenges of Transition

The decision to resign from my position at L&T was not an easy one, nor was it made lightly. Despite numerous discussions with my managers and senior executives who implored me to reconsider my resignation, I remained steadfast in my decision. The persuasive arguments and reassurances from them, aimed at dissuading me from leaving, highlighted their concern but did not alter my resolve. Eventually, my resignation was accepted, and with that, my formal notice period began.

Even my parents were initially resistant to my decision to resign from my job at L&T and embark on the journey of preparing for government exams. It's understandable that parents would be apprehensive about their children leaving a stable job for an uncertain future. To address their concerns, I had to engage in numerous discussions to explain my decision and the reasons behind it. In addition to my parents' concerns, our family was dealing with several financial setbacks at the time. These difficulties stemmed from a series of recent events: my sister's wedding, my grandfather's passing, my father's unemployment, and the broader economic impact of the COVID-19 pandemic. These challenges placed additional pressure on our financial situation, making the prospect of leaving a stable job even more daunting. With such significant pullbacks and uncertainties, reaching a decision that could profoundly impact my future was incredibly challenging.

Balancing my career aspirations with the realities of our family's financial situation required careful consideration and resilience.

The beginning of my notice period marked the start of a significant life transition—from being employed to facing unemployment, and ultimately to diving into preparation for competitive exams. This period of transition was not merely a shift in daily routine but an emotional and psychological shift as well. Leaving behind the familiarity and security of a steady job for the uncertainty of competitive exam preparation was daunting.

Immersing in Exam Preparation

As soon as my notice period commenced, I turned my focus toward preparing for banking exams. This transition involved a steep learning curve. My first step was to familiarize myself with the banking exam syllabus, which seemed dauntingly broad and complex. I began by exploring the syllabus on the IBPS (Institute of Banking Personnel Selection) website, applying for various banking positions to get a sense of the question patterns, and understanding the exam's pressure.

To build a strong foundation, I scoured free resources on YouTube to grasp the concepts required for the exams. This initial phase was crucial as it laid the groundwork for my preparation. My primary focus was on understanding and mastering the concepts of reasoning and quantitative aptitude. I identified two key educational channels that would guide my preparation:

1. **Bankers Adda**: Renowned for its comprehensive coverage of reasoning and quantitative aptitude, this channel featured Saurav Singh Sir as the lecturer for reasoning. His clear and methodical teaching style made complex topics more accessible.

2. **Career Definer**: This channel was pivotal for my quantitative aptitude preparation, led by Kaushik Mohanty Sir. His expertise in quantitative subjects and engaging teaching methods were instrumental in developing a solid understanding of the subject.

I developed a particular admiration for Kaushik Mohanty Sir, whose lectures I found to be exceptionally enlightening. His ability to simplify complex quantitative problems made him a standout instructor. For reasoning, I initially utilized resources from Bankers Adda but later transitioned to Unacademy, where I benefited from the insights of Ankush Lamba Sir. His lectures on reasoning were equally impactful, offering clarity and practical strategies.

Adapting to a New Routine

During my notice period, I chose to work night shifts exclusively. This decision was driven by my desire to study undisturbed during the quieter hours of the night. I dedicated these hours to studying rigorously, focusing primarily on quantitative aptitude and reasoning. Despite the flexibility of my work schedule, the strain of this routine began to take a toll on my health. I experienced significant weight loss and developed dark circles under my eyes, a clear indication of the stress and fatigue I was enduring.

My commitment to studying often led to neglecting my responsibilities at work. Although I made promises to complete assigned tasks, I struggled to meet deadlines. My managers frequently expressed their frustration, suggesting that my inability to handle even minor tasks would hinder my future success. The work environment at L&T was increasingly difficult, with a culture that pressured employees to work long hours and prioritize job demands over work-life balance.

Reflections on Work Culture

The corporate culture at L&T, as I experienced it, was one that seemed to prioritize relentless work hours over effective and intelligent work practices. While management publicly championed work-life balance, the reality was that employees were expected to meet high demands without much regard for their well-being. This disconnect between stated values and actual practices contributed to a stressful work environment and played a significant role in my decision to resign.

The Maruti Suzuki Exam and Its Impact

During this transitional period, I also appeared for the Maruti Suzuki entrance exam. The allure of a lucrative job offer from Maruti Suzuki was a significant distraction. My interview for this position was scheduled for October 18th, 2021 and I traveled to Haryana for the interview, staying in a four-star hotel. The opportunity seemed promising and temporarily diverted my focus from my exam preparation.

Upon returning to Pondicherry, I found myself increasingly preoccupied with waiting for the outcome of the Maruti Suzuki interview. I constantly checked my email, even late into the night, hoping for a notification about my selection or rejection. This fixation on the Maruti Suzuki opportunity led me to neglect my preparation, wasting valuable time during the final month of my notice period.

The last month at L&T was thus marked by a significant lapse in my preparation efforts. I found myself starting from scratch in terms of my exam readiness, having lost precious time that could have been spent studying.

The End of the Notice Period and New Beginnings

My notice period concluded on November 18, 2021, and I packed my belongings to return home on November 27, 2021. This was not just a physical relocation but also a symbolic transition back to the focus of my preparation. I was now poised to restart my journey with renewed determination, despite the setbacks I had encountered.

The prospect of returning home and resuming exam preparation brought with it a mix of hope and apprehension. I was aware of the challenges that lay ahead, including the vast syllabus and the high expectations of my family. The road to securing a government job was fraught with competition, and the odds seemed daunting given the high number of candidates and low success rates.

Gearing Up for the IBPS Clerk Prelims

During my notice period, I had applied for the IBPS Clerk exam, with the prelims scheduled for December 20, 2021. Given my limited preparation time, I focused on covering only the basics of reasoning required for the prelims, using resources from Ankush Lamba Sir's YouTube sessions.

I also completed a mock test modeled after the IBPS Clerk exam pattern. This exercise provided a valuable preview of the exam format and the types of questions that might be asked. On the day of the prelims, I attempted 79 out of 100 questions, a number that I felt reasonably confident about.

Following the exam, the waiting period for the results was tense. I was advised to begin preparing for the mains exam, but the uncertainty of the prelims results made it challenging to fully commit to the next phase of preparation.

When the results were finally announced, I was relieved to learn that I had been selected for the next stage. With a score of 81 out of 100, my performance was above the threshold and indicated that my shift had been more difficult than others. This success was a significant morale booster.

Preparing for the Mains Exam

Buoyed by my prelims success, I directed my efforts towards preparing for the mains exam. Despite knowing that my preparation was incomplete, I invested time in studying, practicing mock tests, and keeping up with current affairs. The mains exam took place on January 25, 2022.

Although my performance in the mains was not as strong as I had hoped, I remained optimistic. The experience had been invaluable, and I was determined to continue improving and preparing for future opportunities.

Final Reflections and Moving Forward

When the results for the IBPS Clerk mains were released on April 1, 2022, I found that I had not been selected, missing the cutoff by just 6 marks. While this was a disappointment, I was proud of the effort I had put into my preparation. The journey had been challenging but also rich in learning experiences.

Final Thoughts for Readers

To anyone embarking on a similar journey, I would say that life is full of opportunities, and the key to success lies in perseverance and dedication. Keep exploring new opportunities, stay focused on your goals, and don't be discouraged by setbacks. The path to achieving your objectives may be fraught with challenges, but with resilience and hard work, you can overcome them and reach your desired destination.

Challenges and Strategies for Overcoming Them

1. Navigating the Emotional Transition from Employment to Unemployment

Challenge: Transitioning from a stable job to a period of unemployment and focusing on exam preparation can be emotionally taxing and stressful. This shift often involves leaving behind a secure routine and facing an uncertain future.

Strategy:

- **Establish a Routine:** Create a structured daily schedule that includes specific times for study, exercise, and relaxation to build a new routine and provide stability.
- **Seek Support:** Discuss your concerns and transition with family, friends, or a mentor to gain emotional support and perspective.
- **Stay Focused on Goals:** Remind yourself of the reasons behind your resignation and the benefits of pursuing a new career path to maintain motivation.

2. Managing Health Issues Due to Irregular Study Hours

Challenge: Adopting a night shift study routine can lead to health problems such as weight loss, fatigue, and disrupted sleep patterns.

Strategy:

- **Prioritize Health:** Balance your study schedule with adequate sleep, healthy eating, and regular physical activity to mitigate health issues.
- **Monitor Well-being:** Pay attention to signs of physical or mental distress and make adjustments to your routine as needed.

- **Use Breaks Wisely:** Incorporate short breaks and relaxation techniques into your study schedule to avoid burnout.

3. Balancing Work Responsibilities with Exam Preparation
Challenge: Struggling to manage work tasks while focusing on exam preparation can lead to decreased productivity, criticism from managers, and job dissatisfaction.
Strategy:

- **Communicate Clearly:** If possible, inform your manager about your study commitments and seek flexibility in your work responsibilities.
- **Time Management:** Use techniques like prioritizing tasks and setting specific study hours to manage both work and preparation efficiently.
- **Maintain Professionalism:** Continue to meet work obligations as best as you can to avoid further criticism and maintain a positive professional reputation.

4. Handling Distractions from New Opportunities
Challenge: The allure of an attractive job offer, such as the one from Maruti Suzuki, can divert attention from exam preparation, leading to procrastination and inefficiencies.
Strategy:

- **Set Boundaries:** Clearly delineate time spent exploring new opportunities versus time dedicated to study to minimize distractions.
- **Reassess Priorities:** Regularly remind yourself of your long-term goals and how current distractions might impact your progress.
- **Stay Organized:** Use tools like calendars or planners to track deadlines and manage your focus on important tasks.

5. Dealing with Setbacks and Missed Cutoffs

Challenge: Experiencing setbacks, such as not passing an exam or missing a cutoff, can be discouraging and impact your motivation.

Strategy:

- **Reflect and Learn:** Analyze the reasons behind the setback and identify areas for improvement. Use this information to refine your study strategy.
- **Stay Positive:** Focus on what you've learned and achieved rather than dwelling on failures. Celebrate small successes to keep up morale.
- **Plan for the Future:** Develop a revised plan for further preparation and set new goals to maintain momentum.

6. Adapting to a New Study Environment

Challenge: Adjusting to a new environment and routine after leaving a corporate job can be challenging, especially when transitioning back to focused exam preparation.

Strategy:

- **Reestablish Routine:** Quickly establish a new study routine and environment that supports focused preparation.
- **Evaluate and Adjust:** Continuously assess your study methods and environment to ensure they align with your current needs and goals.
- **Seek Motivation:** Revisit your initial reasons for pursuing this career change and use them as motivation to stay on track.

Conclusion

Transitioning from a stable job to preparing for competitive exams involves navigating emotional, physical, and professional challenges. By developing a structured routine, prioritizing health, managing distractions, and learning from setbacks, you can overcome these obstacles and stay focused on achieving your career goals. Embrace the journey with resilience and determination, and remember that each challenge is an opportunity for growth and improvement.

Message to Readers

Embarking on a career transition or preparing for competitive exams is a journey filled with both challenges and opportunities. From my experience, I want to share a few key takeaways that might help you on your path:

1. **Stay Focused on Your Goals:** The decision to change your career or pursue new challenges requires unwavering focus. It's essential to keep your long-term objectives in sight, even when faced with temporary distractions or setbacks.

2. **Embrace the Transition:** Moving from a stable job to a period of uncertainty can be daunting. Embrace this transition as an opportunity for growth and self-discovery. A structured approach and a clear plan can make this period more manageable.

3. **Prioritize Your Well-being:** Success is not only about hard work but also about maintaining your health. Balance your study or work routine with self-care to avoid burnout and ensure you stay productive and focused.

4. **Learn from Setbacks:** Facing setbacks is a natural part of any challenging endeavor. Use them as learning experiences to refine your strategies and approach. Every failure or difficulty is a step towards your eventual success.

5. **Be Open to New Opportunities:** Sometimes, unexpected opportunities may arise, and it's okay to explore them. However, it's crucial to assess how these opportunities align with your long-term goals and to manage your focus accordingly.

6. **Reflect and Adapt:** Regularly evaluate your progress and be flexible in adapting your strategies. Reflection helps in recognizing what works best for you and in making necessary adjustments to stay on track.

Remember, perseverance and dedication are key. The journey might be challenging, but with resilience and hard work, you can overcome obstacles and achieve your goals. Embrace each step of the process, and remain committed to your path. Your determination will ultimately lead you to success.

CHAPTER FOURTEEN

Author's View On Corporate Life

Author's Perspective on Corporate Life

The author's experience with corporate life at L&T reveals a complex and often disheartening view of modern work environments. Several key aspects characterize this perspective:

1. **Disconnect Between Values and Practices:** The author notes a significant disparity between the company's publicly promoted values and its actual practices. L&T's public commitment to work-life balance seemed inconsistent with the reality of long working hours and constant pressure. This misalignment between what the company preached and what it practiced contributed to a growing sense of disillusionment.

2. **The Myth of Work-Life Balance:** Despite corporate rhetoric advocating for work-life balance, the author's experience highlighted that the reality often involved grueling hours and high expectations. The ideal of a balanced life was frequently undermined by the demand for extended working hours, leaving employees struggling to manage their personal lives alongside their professional commitments.

3. **Health and Well-being Implications:** The demanding nature of the job took a considerable toll on the author's physical and mental health. The stress of balancing professional responsibilities with personal well-being led to significant

weight loss, dark circles under the eyes, and overall fatigue. This deterioration in health underscored the harsh impact of the corporate culture on employees' lives.

4. **Impact of Corporate Expectations:** The intense focus on meeting deadlines and delivering results often resulted in a work culture where long hours were prioritized over efficiency. This expectation created an environment where employees felt compelled to work beyond reasonable limits, often at the expense of their health and personal lives. The author experienced firsthand how this culture could lead to dissatisfaction and decreased productivity.

5. **Personal Decision to Resign:** The culmination of these challenges led the author to make the difficult decision to resign. The frustration with the work environment, coupled with the adverse effects on health and personal life, made it clear that a change was necessary. The decision to leave was driven by a need to seek a more balanced and fulfilling career path, away from the demands and pressures of the corporate setting.

In summary, the author's reflections on corporate life offer a critique of the often superficial commitment to work-life balance and the real challenges faced by employees. The experience underscores the need for a more authentic approach to supporting employee well-being and aligning corporate practices with the values they espouse.

When someone finds themselves trapped in a corporate job, like the author experienced at L&T, making a decision about whether to stay or leave requires a deep and thorough evaluation of multiple factors. The author's journey provides several critical insights that can guide others in similar situations to make informed decisions that prioritize their well-being and long-term happiness. Here's a detailed exploration of how to navigate such a decision:

1. Identify the Disconnect Between Values and Reality

- **Assess Company Values vs. Practices**: The author experienced a significant disparity between L&T's publicly promoted values, like work-life balance, and the harsh reality of the job, which involved long hours and constant pressure. When assessing your own job, it's essential to critically evaluate whether the company's values align with what is actually practiced. A persistent misalignment can lead to dissatisfaction and should be a key factor in deciding whether to stay or move on.
- **Evaluate Your Own Values**: Understand what matters most to you in a job—be it work-life balance, professional growth, meaningful work, or a supportive environment. Compare these with the company's practices. If there is a disconnect, ask yourself if it's something you can live with or if it's time to consider other opportunities.

2. Understand the Impact on Health and Well-being

- **Monitor Physical and Mental Health**: The author's experience at L&T led to severe health issues, including significant weight loss, dark circles under the eyes, and general fatigue. Prolonged stress and overwork can have detrimental effects on your physical and mental health. If your job is causing such harm, it's a strong indicator that a change is necessary.
- **Recognize Early Warning Signs**: It's important to pay attention to early signs of burnout, such as chronic stress, anxiety, lack of sleep, and physical symptoms like headaches or fatigue. These are signals that your current work environment might be unsustainable, and continuing in such conditions could lead to more serious health problems.

3. Critically Evaluate the Work Culture

- **Examine Expectations vs. Efficiency**: In many corporate environments, like the one described by the author, there is an intense focus on long hours and meeting tight deadlines, often at the expense of efficiency. This can create a culture where employees feel compelled to overwork to meet unrealistic expectations. Reflect on whether this culture is conducive to your productivity and happiness. Are you working long hours because it's necessary, or because it's expected? Is this sustainable in the long run?

- **Consider the Impact on Personal Life**: A demanding job that requires extended working hours can severely impact your personal life, making it difficult to maintain relationships, hobbies, and overall life satisfaction. Consider whether the sacrifices you are making in your personal life are worth the professional gains.

4. Weigh the Decision to Stay or Leave

- **Reflect on Long-Term Goals**: Think about where you see yourself in the next five to ten years. Does your current job align with these aspirations, or is it a hindrance? The author's decision to resign was driven by the realization that staying at L&T was incompatible with the life they wanted to lead. Similarly, consider whether your current role is moving you closer to your goals or keeping you stuck in a place that doesn't serve your long-term interests.
- **Evaluate Financial and Career Implications**: Leaving a job, especially a secure corporate position, can be daunting due to financial and career implications. Before making the leap, consider your financial stability, the availability of other job opportunities, and how leaving might impact your career trajectory. However, remember that no job is worth sacrificing your health and happiness.
- **Explore Alternatives Within the Company**: Before deciding to leave, explore whether there are alternative roles or departments within the company that might better align with your values and needs. Sometimes a change of role or team can make a significant difference.

5. Make a Personal and Informed Decision

- **Trust Your Instincts**: The decision to stay or leave ultimately comes down to your instincts and personal circumstances. The author reached a breaking point where resigning was the best option for their well-being. Trust your gut feelings about whether your current situation is tenable or if a change is necessary.
- **Seek External Advice**: Talk to mentors, colleagues, or friends who might have faced similar dilemmas. Their insights can provide valuable perspectives and help you make a more informed decision.
- **Prepare for the Transition**: If you decide to leave, prepare for the transition by updating your resume, networking, and exploring new opportunities. Having a plan in place can make the process less stressful and more empowering.

6. Focus on a Balanced and Fulfilling Career Path

- **Prioritize Well-being**: Post-resignation, like the author, you might seek a career path that allows for better work-life balance and aligns more closely with your values. This might mean exploring roles in companies with a stronger emphasis on employee well-being, or perhaps pursuing opportunities that offer greater flexibility.
- **Redefine Success**: Consider redefining what success means to you. Instead of viewing success purely in terms of job titles and salaries, consider factors like job satisfaction, personal growth, and quality of life. A fulfilling career is one that aligns with your personal values and allows you to live a balanced and healthy life.

Conclusion

If you find yourself trapped in a corporate job similar to the author's experience at L&T, it's crucial to take a step back and critically evaluate your situation. Prioritize your health and well-being, recognize the signs of a toxic work culture, and make decisions that align with your long-term happiness and career goals. Whether that means staying and seeking changes within the company, or making the bold decision to leave and pursue a new path, the choice should be informed, deliberate, and centered around what's best for your overall life satisfaction.

Part-3

Journey of Preparation for Competitive Exams & Final Appointment as a Government Employee:

This is the third and final part of the book, where the author provides a comprehensive and detailed account of his journey from preparation for competitive exams to finally securing a government job. This section delves deeply into the various aspects of his experience, offering insights into the relentless dedication and resilience required to achieve his goal.

Rigorous Preparation Process

The author begins by recounting the meticulous preparation process he undertook. He outlines the extensive range of exams he appeared for, each with its unique challenges and demands. The book explores the strategies he employed to tackle different subjects, the study materials he relied on, and the rigorous courses he enrolled in to strengthen his understanding and knowledge base.

The author discusses how he meticulously crafted a daily schedule that balanced study time, revision, and practice exams. This schedule was not just about clocking in hours of study but also about optimizing his time to cover the vast syllabus effectively. The preparation process was intense, requiring him to sacrifice personal time, social engagements, and even basic comforts to stay on track.

Daily Struggles and Challenges

One of the key highlights of this part is the discussion of the daily struggles and challenges the author faced throughout his preparation. The author had to wake up at the crack of dawn, often before sunrise, to ensure he had enough time to study before heading to exam centers. These exam centers were not always close by; in fact, many were located nearly 40 kilometers away, requiring long and exhausting commutes.

The journey to these centers was fraught with difficulties. The author describes enduring extreme weather conditions, from the blistering heat of the summer sun to torrential rains and the biting cold of winter mornings. Despite these physical and environmental challenges, the author remained determined and focused on his goal. Each journey to the exam center became a test of his endurance, both mentally and physically, pushing him to his limits but also strengthening his resolve.

Overcoming Obstacles and Achieving Success

In this section, the author provides an honest account of the various obstacles he encountered—not just external, such as harsh weather and long travel, but also internal challenges like self-doubt, fatigue, and the pressure of expectations. He discusses how he managed to stay motivated despite the setbacks and failures he faced along the way, offering readers a candid look at the emotional and psychological toll that such a demanding journey can take.

The author also shares stories of near-misses, where he narrowly missed clearing exams by just a few marks, and how these experiences fueled his determination to try again with even greater vigor. He emphasizes the importance of resilience, perseverance, and maintaining a positive mindset, even in the face of repeated disappointments.

Success and Final Appointment

The culmination of this part of the book is the author's success in clearing multiple government exams, eventually leading to his appointment as a government employee. He recounts the moment when he received the final appointment letter, marking the end of a long and arduous journey and the beginning of a new chapter in his life.

The author reflects on how this achievement was not just about securing a job but about fulfilling a dream he had nurtured since childhood. The sense of pride and satisfaction that came with finally achieving his goal is palpable, as is the acknowledgment of the many sacrifices and struggles that paved the way to his success.

Reflection on the Journey

In the closing chapters of this part, the author offers a reflective analysis of his journey, discussing what he learned about himself and the nature of perseverance. He highlights the importance of setting clear goals, being disciplined, and maintaining unwavering focus, even when the odds seem insurmountable.

The author also provides advice for others who might be on a similar path, sharing practical tips and motivational insights to help them navigate their own challenges. He emphasizes that while the journey to securing a government job is filled with

obstacles, it is ultimately achievable with the right mindset and
dedication.

Conclusion

This third part of the book serves as both a personal narrative and
a guide for aspiring government employees. Through his detailed
recounting of the preparation process, the daily struggles, and the
eventual triumph, the author provides a powerful testament to the
value of hard work, resilience, and the pursuit of one's dreams.
This section not only celebrates the author's achievement but also
serves as an inspiration for anyone facing similar challenges,
encouraging them to keep pushing forward, no matter how
difficult the journey may seem

CHAPTER FIFTEEN

Initial Preparation Days

**As I mentioned in earlier chapters, I resigned from L&T Puducherry on November 18, 2021, and caught my train to Patna on November 27, 2021. I arrived at my hometown the following day, feeling a mix of relief and uncertainty. The decision to leave L&T was not made lightly, but I knew that if I wanted to pursue a career in the government sector, I needed to commit fully to my studies. Before leaving L&T, I had applied for several competitive exams, but the results were disappointing. Out of all the prelims I appeared for, I only managed to pass one—the IBPS Clerk exam. I failed the others, and it didn't take long to realize why. I hadn't yet covered the reasoning syllabus, nor had I taken any practice tests to gauge my preparedness. It was a stark reminder that if I wanted to succeed, I needed to approach my preparation with greater rigor and discipline.

A Wake-Up Call: Realizing the Need for Rigorous Study

The initial failures served as a crucial wake-up call. It became clear that my preparation was lacking, especially in areas like reasoning, quantitative aptitude, English, current affairs, and static general awareness. I knew that to succeed in these competitive exams, I couldn't just rely on self-study. I needed structured guidance. This realization led me to enroll in video lecture courses that would provide me with the necessary knowledge and strategies to tackle these subjects effectively.

My daily routine soon transformed into a relentless pursuit of excellence. I established a demanding schedule that began at 8:00

AM and often stretched well into the night, sometimes until 2:00 or 2:30 AM. This grueling routine became my new normal. However, instead of merely focusing on time spent studying, I adopted a target-oriented approach. Each day, I set specific goals—whether it was completing a set of lectures, mastering a particular concept, or solving a certain number of practice questions.

Building a Routine: Striking a Balance Between Study and Life

My schedule wasn't just about studying all day long. I allocated time for essential activities like bathing, eating, and taking short breaks to recharge. But even these activities were tightly managed to ensure that they didn't interfere with my study targets. It was a tough adjustment, but I knew that without such discipline, achieving my goals would remain a distant dream.

In the beginning, this sudden shift in my lifestyle puzzled those around me. Friends, family members, and neighbors who visited would often ask, "What's happened to him? Why has he suddenly surrounded himself with books, notes, and sticky notes everywhere?" I'm a straightforward person, so I didn't want to leave anyone in doubt, especially when it concerned my life choices. I openly told them that I had resigned from my job and was now dedicating myself to preparing for competitive exams.

Their reactions were mixed. Some were supportive, but many were skeptical. People would joke, saying I was getting too old for marriage and that securing a government job wasn't easy, especially with so many candidates competing for a limited number of positions each year. Even before I resigned, one of my managers had advised me, "Look, Abhishek, you're getting older. You need to think about marriage, so wrap things up as quickly as possible!" But I knew that pursuing my dream was more important than rushing into marriage or settling for something less than what I wanted in life.

A Personal Story: Choosing Between Marriage and Career

Before I delve deeper into my preparation journey, I want to share a personal story that illustrates the tough choices I had to make. While I was still working at L&T, my parents began receiving several marriage proposals for me. Among them, there was one that my family and I initially favored. I even started communicating with the girl, but deep down, I knew something wasn't right. My gut told me that pursuing this marriage could derail my dreams of preparing for and succeeding in government exams.

From a young age, I had always envisioned myself leaving the corporate world to secure a government job—a career that I believed would bring stability and satisfaction. The thought of marriage at that time felt like a potential distraction from my goals. I knew that if I got married, I might not be able to fully commit to my studies, and that thought terrified me. I feared that neither of us would be truly happy if I sacrificed my dreams.

As much as I wanted to be honest with the girl, I struggled to find the courage to tell her the truth. But then something happened at work that pushed me to make a decision. One day, my manager reprimanded me harshly in front of some of the workmen. It was humiliating, but it also served as a catalyst. That day, I realized I couldn't continue living a life that didn't align with my aspirations. I finally gathered the courage to tell the girl that I wasn't ready for marriage and that I wanted to focus on my studies.

Her family tried to convince me otherwise. They assured me that I could continue pursuing my dreams even after marriage and that they would support me financially if needed. But I knew deep down that this wasn't just about money or support; it was about mental space and the freedom to focus entirely on my goals. So, I politely but firmly declined their offer. Looking back, I believe I made the right decision for both of us. She likely found someone better suited for her, and I eventually found happiness and fulfillment in my own life. Today, I'm happily married to my wife, Bineeta, and I'm working in a government job that brings me peace and stability—something I never felt while I was at L&T.

The Preparation Journey Begins

Now, let me take you back to my preparation journey:

1. Quantitative Aptitude: I knew that mastering quantitative aptitude was crucial for passing any government exam, especially banking exams. I started by focusing on the arithmetic portion, which I completed through YouTube sessions led by Kaushik Mohanty Sir. His lectures were clear and comprehensive, helping me build a strong foundation in topics like percentages, profit and loss, time and work, and other essential arithmetic concepts.

However, I still had to cover the miscellaneous topics in speed maths, such as simplification tricks, data interpretation techniques, and number series. These topics are vital for banking exams, where time management is key. To tackle these areas, I enrolled in Kaushik Mohanty Sir's courses on Unacademy, where I learned valuable techniques that would later prove essential in the exams.

2. Analytical Reasoning: Reasoning is another critical component of competitive exams. Although I had a basic understanding of the reasoning syllabus for prelims, I realized that I needed more in-depth knowledge and practice. I decided to take a full course from Ankush Lamba Sir, who is well-known for his reasoning classes.

Under his guidance, I learned various techniques for solving different types of reasoning problems, including syllogisms, sequence-based problems, direction tests, blood relation puzzles, inequalities, alphabetical series, seating arrangements, and puzzles. I spent a significant amount of time practicing puzzles, which are often the most challenging part of the reasoning section. It took about two months of consistent effort to master these concepts and develop the speed and accuracy needed for the exams.

3. English: English is a unique section in banking exams, where the focus is more on comprehension skills rather than grammar. Initially, I was worried that I would need extensive grammar lessons, as many YouTube teachers suggested. But over time, I realized that these teachers were promoting their courses more as a business rather than offering practical advice.

The truth is, if your comprehension skills are strong, you don't need to invest heavily in grammar lessons. Instead, I focused on improving my reading and comprehension skills by dedicating an hour each day to reading editorial sections from newspapers. This practice not only enhanced my understanding of complex texts but also improved my vocabulary and reading speed—both of which are crucial for performing well in the English section of the exams.

4. Current Affairs & Static General Knowledge: For current affairs and static GK, I followed the Banker's Adda channel with Ashish Gautam Sir. He provided a solid foundation in both current events and static topics. However, I noticed that sometimes his coverage of current affairs wasn't detailed enough for my needs, so I supplemented his teachings with daily and monthly PDFs from Affairs Cloud. These resources helped me stay updated with the latest events and ensured that I had a comprehensive understanding of both current and static knowledge required for the exams.

The Results of Hard Work: Seeing Improvement and New Opportunities

After rigorously following this study plan for two and a half months, I began to see significant improvements in my mock exam scores. My percentile scores in practice tests soared above 90%, giving me a newfound confidence that I was on the right path. Around December 2021, just as I was preparing for the IBPS Clerk exams, another opportunity presented itself: a notification from ESIC (Employees' State Insurance Corporation) about upcoming exams.

The ESIC exam pattern was similar to banking exams, with one major difference: the general awareness section placed a greater emphasis on static GK rather than current affairs. This new challenge excited me, as it was another chance to prove myself and potentially secure a government job. The timing was perfect—the exams were scheduled for the first half of 2022, giving me a fresh goal to aim for.

While I was traveling through Jharkhand, enjoying the road trip, I received the ESIC notification. It was a moment of serendipity, as I was already in high spirits from the journey. The notification gave me an extra boost of motivation. As soon as I returned home, the first thing I did was fill out the application form for the ESIC exam.

However, in my excitement, I made a significant mistake during the application process—a blunder that would later cause me considerable stress and anxiety. But I'll save that story for the next chapter.

In the passage, the author describes the challenges faced during the transition from a corporate job at L&T to preparing for competitive government exams. The challenges and ways to tackle them are outlined as follows:

1. Initial Failures and Realization:

- **Challenge:** The author initially failed in most of the preliminary exams attempted, except for the IBPS Clerk exam. This was due to incomplete coverage of the reasoning syllabus and lack of practice tests.
- **Solution:** The author realized the need for rigorous study and structured guidance. To tackle this, the author enrolled in video lecture courses and adopted a target-oriented study routine, which was essential to cover the gaps in knowledge.

2. Establishing a Rigorous Study Routine:

- **Challenge:** The author needed to create a disciplined study routine to cover multiple subjects (reasoning, quantitative aptitude, English, current affairs, and static general knowledge).
- **Solution:** The author developed a demanding daily schedule, starting at 8:00 AM and often lasting until 2:00 or 2:30 AM. The study plan was target-oriented, with specific goals set for each day, such as completing lectures, practicing questions, and balancing study time with essential daily activities.

3. Social Pressure and Skepticism:

- **Challenge:** The author faced skepticism and social pressure from family and acquaintances who questioned the decision to resign from a stable job and focus on competitive exams, especially at an age when marriage was also a societal expectation.

- **Solution:** The author remained transparent about the goals, clearly communicating the decision to prepare for exams. Despite the ridicule and doubts from others, the author stayed focused on the long-term goal of securing a government job.

4. Personal Sacrifices and Decision-Making:

- **Challenge:** The author had to choose between pursuing marriage and focusing on career goals. This decision was complicated by a proposal that the family had initially accepted.
- **Solution:** The author prioritized career ambitions over marriage, understanding that marriage could potentially distract from the preparation for government exams. This decision was made after reflecting on personal goals and the long-term impact on happiness and career satisfaction.

5. Mastering Specific Subjects:

- **Quantitative Aptitude:**

  - **Challenge:** The author needed to master the arithmetic and miscellaneous portions of quantitative aptitude.
  - **Solution:** The author followed YouTube sessions by Kaushik Mohanty Sir and Unacademy courses to learn simplification tricks, data interpretation, and number series, which were crucial for banking exams.

- **Analytical Reasoning:**

  - **Challenge:** The author needed to develop strong reasoning skills, especially for puzzle-based problems that are common in competitive exams.

- **Solution:** The author took a full reasoning course from Ankush Lamba Sir and dedicated significant time to practicing puzzles and other reasoning topics, taking about two months to cover all concepts.

- **English:**

  - **Challenge:** The author was initially concerned about needing extensive grammar lessons.
  - **Solution:** The author realized that strong comprehension skills were more important for banking exams and focused on reading newspaper editorials daily to improve English skills.

- **Current Affairs & Static General Knowledge:**

  - **Challenge:** The author needed to stay updated with current affairs and static GK, which are critical for competitive exams.
  - **Solution:** The author followed Ashish Gautam Sir on Banker's Adda for a solid foundation and supplemented it with daily and monthly PDFs from Affairs Cloud to cover the topics in detail.

6. Dealing with Exam Notifications and Mistakes:

- **Challenge:** The author made a significant mistake while filling out the application form for the ESIC exam.
- **Solution:** While the specific mistake is not detailed in this passage, the author hints at the importance of attention to detail during the application process, which will be discussed further in the next chapter.

A Message to My Readers: Cherishing the Right Decisions:

Encouragement: The author encourages readers to reflect on and take pride in the tough decisions they make in life, emphasizing that the right choices, made with conviction, will never lead to regret. The author urges readers to maintain hope and faith in their decisions.

Life is full of choices, and some decisions will make you feel proud for years to come. Whether it's choosing to focus on your career, turning down an opportunity that doesn't align with your goals, or deciding to take the plunge into the unknown, these moments shape who you are. Cherish those decisions, and let them remind you that hope and determination will guide you through life's challenges. Never lose faith in your ability to make the right choices.

In **summary**, the author describes various challenges encountered during the transition from a corporate job to preparing for government exams. Each challenge is met with thoughtful solutions, rooted in discipline, self-awareness, and a clear focus on long-term goals.

Happy reading!!

CHAPTER SIXTEEN

Form Filling Of ESIC & Final Selection

Application for the ESIC Exam: After returning from my trip to the scenic landscapes of Jharkhand, where I spent time exploring nature and reflecting on my goals, I felt a renewed sense of determination. I promptly applied for the ESIC (Employees' State Insurance Corporation) exam through their official website. This was a crucial step in my career journey, as I aimed to secure a stable government position. I applied under the EWS (Economically Weaker Section) category, which mandated a valid EWS certificate for the financial year relevant to my exam application.

Regrettably, the EWS certificate I possessed was from the previous financial year, and I was unaware at the time that I needed to obtain an updated certificate for the current financial year. I felt a surge of anxiety as I realized the importance of this detail. The application form clearly stated that all reservation certificates must be dated on or before the closing date of the application form. This crucial information came to light while engaging with fellow aspirants in various Telegram groups, where students actively shared their insights and experiences.

The conversations in these groups heightened my concern, and I began to fear that my application might face rejection during the document verification process. To address the situation, I took proactive steps and secured a new EWS certificate for the correct financial year (FY 2022-23). However, in a twist of fate, the certificate was issued after the closing date of the application form.

In my quest for reassurance, I sought advice from multiple individuals. Some provided guidance that bolstered my hope, while others raised doubts about the validity of my application. This conflicting advice left me in a state of uncertainty, and the fear of rejection loomed large in my mind. Ultimately, I decided to surrender the outcome to fate, channeling my energy into rigorous preparation, determined not to let these challenges derail my focus.

Prelims Examination: The prelims exam was scheduled for March 19, 2022, coinciding with the vibrant festival of Holi, a time when colors filled the air and joy enveloped the streets. As people celebrated with family and friends, I was on my way to the examination center, navigating roads adorned with vibrant colors and festive decorations. While others indulged in the festivities, my mind was preoccupied with the upcoming exam and the weight of responsibility I felt for my family.

Upon entering the examination hall, I observed a diverse range of emotions among my fellow candidates—some engaged in animated discussions about potential questions, while others sat in contemplative silence, lost in their thoughts. I proceeded with the verification process, where my identity was confirmed through biometric checks, and I signed the attendance sheet with a mixture of excitement and apprehension.

After settling into my designated seat, I powered on the computer, ensuring all systems were functioning correctly. I took a deep breath and mentally strategized my approach for the exam, aiming to attempt over 90 questions out of the 100 presented. As the exam commenced, following the invigilator's instructions, I felt a surge of adrenaline. I was ready to tackle the challenge ahead.

Throughout the exam, I maintained my focus and was able to attempt 96 questions. Each correct answer carried 2 marks, while incorrect responses incurred a 0.5 mark penalty. With a sense of accomplishment, I returned home after the exam, where my father eagerly awaited my return. He stood outside the examination hall, his face filled with curiosity. When he asked me how many questions I had attempted, a wave of relief washed over me as I shared my results, and his satisfaction with my response brought a sense of pride.

Result Announcement: Instead of dwelling on the anxiety of waiting for the prelims results, I chose to channel my energy into preparing for the mains examination. My determination to succeed only grew stronger. The result was announced on the night of April 14 or 15, 2022. I eagerly awaited the news, and when it was finally released, I was ecstatic to find out that I had scored 164.5 marks in the prelims. The announcement came late in the evening, around 11 PM, and my heart raced with excitement.

In a moment of sheer joy, I rushed to my parents' room, waking them from their slumber to share the incredible news. Their expressions transformed from confusion to elation as I informed them that I had successfully cleared the prelims and would be moving on to the next stage of the examination process.

Mains Preparation: With a newfound sense of purpose, I dove headfirst into preparing for the mains exam. The intensity of my studies ramped up significantly. I enrolled in numerous mock test series, each designed to simulate the real exam environment, which provided invaluable practice. I meticulously covered all relevant topics, with a particular emphasis on current affairs from the previous five months. Multiple revisions were crucial to ensure I retained the information.

In addition to current affairs, I practiced puzzles and other critical topics that often appeared in competitive exams. I maintained a disciplined study schedule, while also keeping an eye on other examinations to diversify my opportunities.

An unexpected challenge arose just days before the scheduled mains examination. My cousin's wedding was set for April 27, 2022, a mere three days before my mains exam on April 30, 2022. This timing presented a dilemma; I had resigned from my previous job to focus entirely on preparing for government exams, and the thought of attending a wedding while my peers celebrated their achievements weighed heavily on my mind. I imagined encountering relatives who would inquire about my career progress, and I dreaded the inevitable question: "What are you doing these days?"

I knew that attending the ceremony would lead to distractions and potentially negative thoughts that could affect my focus before the exam. After much contemplation, I made the difficult decision to skip the wedding, prioritizing my studies over social obligations. This decision was met with disappointment from family members, leading to internal conflicts and some resentment. However, I remained steadfast in my resolve, understanding that I had to protect my mental state and maintain a positive outlook before the exam.

Date of Mains Examination: The mains exam was set for April 30, 2022. The day before, anxiety gripped me, compounded by disruptions in my study routine caused by several weddings taking place in the neighborhood. In our culture, weddings are celebrated with loud music played on DJ trolleys, creating an exuberant atmosphere that made concentration nearly impossible. The cacophony of sound reverberated through my home, distracting me from my revisions and leaving me frazzled.

The night before the exam, I found myself unable to sleep, thoughts racing through my mind as I prepared for the challenges ahead. Finally, at 4:30 AM, I decided to rise, feeling a mix of anticipation and trepidation. My father and I set out at 6:00 AM, embarking on the journey from our home to the examination center.

However, another stroke of misfortune awaited me at the exam hall. After successfully completing the verification checks, I discovered that the roll number on my admit card was not printed clearly. This was a critical issue, as I needed to enter my roll number as a password to access the exam server. When I attempted to log in, I faced repeated error messages, which only heightened my anxiety.

I called the invigilator for assistance, and she guided me through the process of entering the numbers. Despite her help, the error persisted. Frustration began to creep in as I realized that my confidence was already wavering before the exam had even begun. Eventually, the invigilator took my admit card to confirm the roll number with her superiors. They verified that the roll number was indeed correct, but the initial hiccup had already shattered much of my confidence.

Despite the challenges I faced, I managed to maintain my composure. The exam commenced, and I was pleasantly surprised to find that the general awareness section, which previously focused on static General Knowledge questions in the 2019 paper, was now heavily weighted towards current affairs—my area of strength. My extensive preparation paid off, and I felt a surge of confidence as I tackled each section of the exam.

Overall, I attempted 176 questions out of 200, with each question carrying 1 mark and a penalty of 0.25 marks for incorrect answers. While the exam went well, I reflected on the fact that I could have attempted 5-7 more questions had I not gotten stuck on a particularly challenging puzzle. Nevertheless, I was satisfied with my performance and felt I had done my best.

Result of Mains: The results for the mains exam were announced on June 16, 2022. I felt a mix of excitement and apprehension as I logged in to check my score. To my delight, I had scored 167.25 marks out of 200—a result that confirmed my hard work and dedication had paid off. My father, who had been sitting next to me, shared in my joy as we celebrated this significant milestone.

However, I knew that while the mains score was crucial, my selection was not yet guaranteed, as there was still a third phase to complete. I felt a sense of optimism and confidence in my performance, so I devised techniques to estimate my chances of selection and prepared for the final phase of the process.

Phase-III's Preparation and Selection: Phase-III consisted of a skill test, assessing my proficiency in essential computer applications such as Excel, Word, and PowerPoint. I had diligently prepared for this test, practicing extensively to ensure I was well-versed in each application. When the time for the skill test arrived, I felt confident and ready. I approached the test with a calm mindset, and to my satisfaction, I scored 49 out of 50 marks—a testament to my hard work and preparation.

Although the final merit list would not be released until December 2022, I felt a sense of accomplishment knowing that I had put forth my best effort and performed exceptionally well. The anticipation was bittersweet, as I eagerly awaited confirmation of my selection.

One More Selection Apart from ESIC UDC: In addition to the UDC (Upper Division Clerk) position, ESIC had announced notifications for three posts, and I had applied for two of them—the UDC and the MTS (Multi-Tasking Staff) positions. The MTS exam was conducted in parallel with the UDC exam, with two phases. I worked hard for both exams, and when the results were announced, I was elated to find that I had been selected for the MTS position as well.

Since the selection process for MTS was shorter than that of UDC, I received my joining letter earlier and joined ESIC as an MTS on November 18, 2022—exactly one year after I had resigned from L&T on November 18, 2021. This transition marked a pivotal moment in my career journey, as I had finally secured a stable government position, a goal I had pursued with unwavering determination.

However, my journey didn't end there. On February 6, 2023, I made the decision to resign from the MTS position, feeling it was the right time to pursue my ambition further. Just a few days later, on February 14, 2023, I joined as a UDC. This transition was not only significant for my career but also marked my entry into a government role governed by central government pay rules—a milestone I had worked tirelessly to achieve.

As I reflect on those challenging days, I am reminded that hard work, perseverance, and making difficult choices truly pay off. The struggles, sacrifices, and decisions I made along the way were all worth it, ultimately leading me to a stable and fulfilling career as a government employee. I now carry the lessons learned from this journey with me, using them as motivation to continue striving for excellence in my professional life.

Message to Readers:

Dear Readers,

As I reflect on my journey through the ESIC examination process, I want to share some key lessons and experiences that may resonate with you, especially if you're navigating similar challenges in pursuit of your goals. This journey was not just about passing exams; it was about personal growth, resilience, and the importance of unwavering determination.

1. The Importance of Preparation: My journey began with a decision to apply for the ESIC exam, a crucial step toward achieving my career aspirations. This decision came after a period of introspection during my trip to the scenic landscapes of Jharkhand, where I reflected on my goals and ambitions. The clarity I gained from this experience fueled my determination to prepare thoroughly for the exams ahead. I learned that preparation is key to success; it involves not only studying the material but also understanding the requirements and processes involved.

2. Overcoming Obstacles: Facing obstacles is a natural part of any journey, and mine was no exception. The realization that my EWS certificate was outdated filled me with anxiety. However, instead of allowing this setback to deter me, I took proactive steps to secure the correct documentation. This experience taught me that challenges can often serve as valuable learning opportunities, pushing us to adapt and find solutions. When I encountered conflicting advice regarding my application, I learned the importance of trusting my instincts and focusing on what I could control: my preparation.

3. Managing Anxiety: The lead-up to the exams was filled with anxiety and uncertainty. Whether it was the noise of celebrations around me or the technical issues on exam day, I had to navigate my feelings and stay focused. I realized that anxiety is a common experience, but how we manage it can make a significant difference. By channeling my energy into preparation rather than dwelling on fears, I found a sense of empowerment. Developing a mindset that embraces challenges rather than fearing them became crucial in maintaining my composure.

4. The Value of Support: Throughout this journey, I found solace in the support of my family and fellow aspirants. My father's unwavering encouragement was a constant source of motivation, reminding me of the importance of having a strong support system. Engaging with others in Telegram groups also provided a sense of community and shared purpose. It reinforced my belief that we don't have to navigate our journeys alone; the support and insights from others can be incredibly valuable.

5. Making Sacrifices: I faced a significant decision when my cousin's wedding coincided with my exam preparations. I chose to prioritize my studies over attending the wedding, understanding that sacrifices are sometimes necessary for the pursuit of our goals. While this decision was met with disappointment from family members, I learned the importance of staying true to my commitments and focusing on what truly mattered to me at that moment. It's essential to evaluate our priorities and make choices that align with our long-term goals, even if they are difficult in the short term.

6. Resilience in the Face of Challenges: The exams themselves were filled with unexpected hurdles, from technical issues during the mains exam to the distractions of weddings nearby. However, I learned that resilience is about maintaining a positive mindset and finding ways to overcome difficulties. When I faced challenges, I reminded myself that every obstacle is an opportunity to grow stronger and more adaptable.

7. Celebrating Achievements: When I finally received my results, the joy I felt was immense—not just for my scores but for the culmination of hard work, determination, and perseverance. Celebrating our achievements, big or small, is crucial in recognizing our efforts and motivating us for future challenges. Sharing my success with my family added to the joy, reinforcing the importance of gratitude and connection along the journey.

8. Continuous Growth: Finally, my journey didn't end with securing a position; I made the decision to resign from the MTS position to pursue further opportunities as a UDC. This transition marked a significant milestone in my career, illustrating the importance of continuous growth and pursuing paths that align with our aspirations. Life is a journey of learning, and each experience shapes us for the next step.

In closing, I hope my story serves as an inspiration for you all. Whether you are preparing for exams, facing personal challenges, or pursuing your career goals, remember that perseverance, adaptability, and a commitment to your aspirations can lead to success. Embrace the journey, celebrate your progress, and trust in your abilities.

Thank you for allowing me to share my experiences with you. I wish each of you the best in your own journeys, and may you find the courage and determination to overcome any obstacles you encounter.

With warm regards,

[Abhishek Kumar Singh]

CHAPTER SEVENTEEN

My Journey With FCI & Some Other Selections

I won't delve into extensive details about my preparation process, as the overall approach is largely similar across various examinations. However, I would like to share my journey during the preparation for the Phase-3 exam of the Upper Division Clerk (UDC) position. During this time, I also decided to apply for a position with the Food Corporation of India (FCI). The preliminary examination for the FCI was conducted in January 2023, and I was stationed in Delhi with the Employees' State Insurance Corporation (ESIC) at that time.

The preliminary exam took place in an examination hall located near Connaught Place, a bustling area in Delhi. On the day of the exam, I felt a mix of excitement and nerves. Although I attempted a decent number of questions, I couldn't recall the exact number as I was preoccupied with my surroundings and the atmosphere of the exam hall. At this point in my life, my preparation for these examinations was somewhat casual. I was savoring different phases of life, exploring the vibrant streets of Delhi, and enjoying my work at ESIC. Everything seemed to be under control, and I felt a sense of comfort in my current job. This comfort, however, led to a lack of rigorous study and preparation for the exams.

To my surprise, I received the news that I had cleared the prelims exam. In addition to the FCI application, I had also participated in the Junior Court Assistant (JCA) examination conducted by the Supreme Court. I successfully cleared the Phase-I of the JCA exam as well. I also cleared the Phase-I of Small Industries Development Bank of India (SIDBI) in this period but failed by few marks in the final list. This period of my life was marked by a sense of achievement and anticipation as I navigated through different opportunities.

Shortly after, I tackled the Phase-2 exam for FCI. The exam was challenging yet rewarding, and I felt satisfied with my performance. Meanwhile, the results for the IBPS PO preliminary exam were announced, and I discovered that I had also been selected there. The excitement of progressing in multiple exams fueled my motivation, but it was short-lived. Although I was successful in the FCI Phase-2 examination, I encountered disappointment when the results for the IBPS PO mains were declared. I fell short by a few marks, largely due to my lack of preparation in current affairs. The sectional cutoff for that part of the exam was relatively easy to score in, yet I managed only 4 marks, which was insufficient to advance further.

Despite this setback, I received an offer letter from FCI for a position in the Bihar region, which filled me with immense joy. Being posted closer to my hometown was a significant milestone for me, as it meant returning to my roots. In light of this new opportunity, I made the decision to forgo the Phase-2 exam for the Supreme Court JCA, choosing instead to focus on my upcoming role at FCI.

On August 5, 2023, I officially resigned from my position as a UDC and joined FCI as a Regional Officer in Patna. The transition was exhilarating. For the first month, my colleagues and I stayed in Patna, where we forged new friendships and got to know one another better. It was a time of bonding and camaraderie as we navigated the initial stages of our new roles together.

In September 2023, we received our assigned posting locations, and I was thrilled to find out that I had been assigned to the Muzaffarpur district. This was a relief, as it placed me only 70 kilometers from my hometown. I felt a sense of satisfaction with my initial posting, knowing I could maintain close ties with my family and community while embarking on this new chapter in my career.

Currently, I am genuinely happy with my job at FCI. The position not only offers a decent salary package but also allows me to find a state of peace and fulfillment in my professional life. Reflecting on this journey, I recognize the importance of adaptability and the willingness to seize opportunities as they arise. The experiences I've had, from preparing for various exams to navigating the job application process, have equipped me with valuable lessons about perseverance and making choices that align with my goals and aspirations.

Message to Readers:

Life is an intricate journey, marked by both challenges and opportunities that shape our paths. My experience transitioning from the Employees' State Insurance Corporation (ESIC) to the Food Corporation of India (FCI) has been a testament to the power of resilience, adaptability, and the importance of making thoughtful choices that align with one's values.

Embracing Change and Adaptability: Throughout my preparation for various examinations, I encountered numerous twists and turns that taught me valuable lessons about life and work. As I navigated the competitive landscape of government examinations, I realized that while dedication and preparation are crucial, it is equally important to embrace the changes life throws our way. My decision to apply for the FCI while balancing my responsibilities at ESIC exemplified my willingness to adapt to new opportunities. It reminded me that growth often comes from stepping outside our comfort zones and exploring new paths.

The Balance Between Work and Life: During my time in Delhi, I found myself enjoying the vibrant atmosphere of the city, yet I also understood the significance of maintaining focus on my goals.

The preparation phase for the examinations was a mix of hard work and personal enjoyment. I had to grapple with the challenge of staying updated on current affairs while balancing my job and social life. It was a delicate dance, but it highlighted the importance of setting priorities and finding a balance between professional aspirations and personal fulfillment.

Learning from Setbacks: Every journey has its hurdles, and mine was no exception. My experience of being selected in the FCI prelims while narrowly missing the IBPS PO mains cutoff taught me valuable lessons in resilience. Although I had prepared extensively, my lack of focus on current affairs became a learning point. This setback reinforced the importance of consistent preparation and being aware of all aspects of the competitive landscape. Each failure is an opportunity to learn and grow, and I embraced that mindset wholeheartedly.

Following Your Roots: Receiving the offer to work in the Bihar region was a significant moment for me. It was not just a job opportunity; it represented a chance to return to my roots, to be closer to my family, and to embrace the familiar comforts of home. The joy of being posted in my native region filled me with a sense of purpose and belonging. It taught me that while career advancement is important, it should not come at the expense of personal happiness and fulfillment. Sometimes, the best choice is the one that aligns with our values and brings us closer to what truly matters.

A Sense of Peace and Fulfillment: As I settled into my role in Muzaffarpur, I felt an overwhelming sense of satisfaction and peace. The transition from UDC to FCI RO Patna was not just a career move; it was a step toward a fulfilling life. I forged new friendships, developed camaraderie with my colleagues, and found joy in my work. This experience taught me that success is not just measured by titles or salary but by the relationships we build and the positive impact we make in our communities.

Encouragement for Others: To anyone reading this, I want to emphasize that your journey is uniquely yours. Embrace the challenges you encounter, learn from your experiences, and make decisions that resonate with your core values. Life will present uncertainties, but it is through navigating those uncertainties that we discover our true potential. Keep pushing forward, stay motivated, and maintain a curious and open mindset.

Remember that every step, whether it feels like progress or a setback, contributes to your growth and development. Trust the process, celebrate your victories—big and small—and never lose sight of what makes you happy. Ultimately, your journey is about more than just reaching a destination; it's about the experiences you gather and the person you become along the way.

May you all find the strength to pursue your dreams and the wisdom to navigate the challenges that come your way.

CHAPTER EIGHTEEN

Life At Government Offices

Author's experience at various government offices:

Since transitioning to my current role, I've experienced a significant reduction in stress, thanks to the mental peace and stability I've achieved. I now enjoy a well-balanced work-life routine, which has greatly enhanced my overall quality of life. My current job allows me to maintain clear boundaries between work and personal time. I make it a point not to bring work home, ensuring that I can fully enjoy my time with family and friends. I complete any tasks left unfinished at the office the following day, which helps me avoid work-related stress during my personal time.

At work, I often find myself with some free moments that I use to browse through reels, chat with friends, or engage in light-hearted office gossip. The absence of strict daily targets has relieved me from the constant pressure of meeting deadlines. Additionally, I appreciate the flexibility of being able to arrive at the office a bit later on certain days without any issues. Being stationed close to my hometown has simplified my commute, eliminating the previous hassle of long journeys and making travel convenient.

Another significant improvement is the ample leave balance I now have, which alleviates any concerns about taking time off when needed. Moreover, the availability of overtime compensation is a welcome change. In my previous role at L&T, I often worked more than 10 hours a day without any additional pay, and there were times when my workdays extended to 15-16 hours. In contrast, my current position provides fair compensation for any extra hours worked beyond the standard schedule.

My personal life has greatly benefited from this improved work-life balance. I feel genuinely relaxed and at ease when I'm at home or in my personal space. With more free time, I've been able to indulge in my hobbies and personal interests. For example, I now have the time to watch a variety of Netflix series, experiment with cooking my favorite meals, and regularly visit the theatre with my wife and family on weekends to enjoy newly released movies—activities that were previously constrained by my demanding work schedule at L&T.

Reflecting on my past experiences, I used to return to my room in Pondicherry around 11:00 PM, leaving me only enough time for a quick dinner before heading to bed. In contrast, my work at various government offices—such as ESIC RO Delhi, ESIC Hospital in Jhilmil, Delhi, FCI RO Patna, and ultimately at a FCI Depot—has consistently provided a similar level of freedom and a supportive work environment.

Working in the government sector not only offers enhanced retirement benefits but also promotes a healthier work culture throughout one's career. This environment supports a healthier heart and a sound mind, contributing to overall well-being. On the other hand, target-oriented roles, with their constant pressure for promotions, appraisals, and bonuses, can lead to chronic stress and various health issues over time.

In the following sections, I will delve deeper into the general benefits of government employment. I hope these insights inspire and motivate those preparing for government exams, despite the challenging competition and rigorous selection process.

General Aspects of life in government offices:

1. Job Security and Stability

- **Employment Longevity:** Government jobs are widely perceived as secure and stable career paths. Unlike many private-sector roles, which may be subject to market fluctuations or economic downturns, government positions typically offer a stable employment environment. This stability appeals to individuals who value a predictable and secure career trajectory. Employees can plan long-term life goals, such as buying a home or saving for their children's education, with confidence that their job is secure.

- **Retirement Benefits:** Government employees benefit from comprehensive retirement packages, which often include pensions through schemes like UPS (Unified Pension Scheme) or NPS (National Pension System). These pensions provide a steady income after retirement, which is often supplemented by gratuities or lump-sum payments. This financial security in retirement is a significant advantage and a key reason why many people choose government careers. The prospect of a secure and well-supported retirement contributes to job satisfaction and long-term career planning.

- **Medical Benefits for Dependents:** Government employees typically enjoy substantial medical benefits, which often extend to their dependents. These benefits can include free medical treatments and consultations at renowned private hospitals, which is a considerable advantage. Access to high-quality medical care without significant out-of-pocket expenses enhances overall job satisfaction and provides peace of mind regarding the health and well-being of family members.

- **Overtime Allowance (OTA):** Government employees who work beyond standard office hours are compensated with an overtime allowance. This additional pay for extra hours worked not only serves as financial compensation but also acknowledges the employee's commitment and extra effort. This benefit helps maintain morale and incentivizes employees to manage workload peaks effectively.

- **Periodic Pay Revisions:** Regular salary increments are a hallmark of government jobs. Employees typically receive three increments per year, which ensures steady salary growth and keeps pace with inflation and cost of living adjustments. This structured approach to salary increases supports financial stability and career progression.

2. Work Culture and Environment

- **Hierarchical Structure:** Government offices often operate with a well-defined hierarchical structure. This includes clear delineation of roles, responsibilities, and authority levels. Such a structure facilitates clear reporting lines and decision-making processes, which helps employees understand their place within the organization and ensures that tasks and responsibilities are allocated effectively. It also aids in maintaining order and clarity in communication, which is crucial in large organizations.
- **Standard Operating Procedures (SOPs):** Employees in government offices work within established Standard Operating Procedures (SOPs), which are designed to maintain consistency and accountability. SOPs outline the protocols for various tasks and decisions, providing a standardized approach to work. While this consistency can improve efficiency and reliability, it may also limit the flexibility and creativity of employees in addressing unique or unforeseen challenges.

3. Work-Life Balance

- **Predictable Schedules:** Government jobs typically offer predictable working hours, with standard office times and minimal overtime requirements. This predictability allows employees to maintain a healthy work-life balance, as they can plan their personal and family activities around their fixed work schedule. This is in contrast to private sector roles where irregular hours and high project demands can encroach on personal time.
- **Family-Friendly Policies:** Many government agencies implement policies that support family life, such as parental

leave, flexible working hours, and telecommuting options. These policies help employees manage their family responsibilities while maintaining their professional roles. For example, parental leave allows new parents to spend time with their newborns without the stress of balancing work demands, and flexible working hours enable employees to accommodate personal commitments.

- **Sports Tournaments:** Some government organizations organize sports tournaments or fitness programs to encourage employees to engage in physical activities. These events promote health and wellness, offering employees a chance to socialize with colleagues outside of the work environment and contribute to their overall fitness and well-being.

4. Professional Development Opportunities

- **Continuous Learning:** Government offices often prioritize employee development by offering a range of training programs, workshops, and seminars. These learning opportunities help employees stay current with evolving policies, regulations, and industry best practices. Continuous learning is vital for career advancement and ensures that employees can effectively contribute to their roles and adapt to changes in their field.

- **Mentorship Programs:** Many government agencies have mentorship programs designed to connect less experienced employees with seasoned professionals. These programs provide guidance and support, helping junior staff navigate their careers, develop skills, and gain insights from experienced mentors. Mentorship can accelerate professional growth and enhance job satisfaction by providing personalized career development advice.

5. Public Service Orientation

- **Commitment to Community:** Government employees often have a deep sense of duty toward public service. This commitment is reflected in their participation in various community outreach initiatives, public health campaigns, and disaster response efforts. Engaging in these activities fosters a sense of fulfillment and pride, as employees contribute directly to the betterment of society.
- **Impactful Projects:** Government employees often work on projects that have a direct impact on citizens' lives, such as infrastructure development, educational reforms, and healthcare access, which can provide a profound sense of fulfillment. For instance, in the Food Corporation of India (FCI), employees contribute to public welfare by ensuring each household receives 5 kg of free ration per person per month. Similarly, in the Employees' State Insurance Corporation (ESIC), employees facilitate medical benefits and insurance at a minimal rate, with contributions of 0.75% from the employee and 3.25% from the employer for those earning up to Rs. 21,000 per month

6. Challenges and Bureaucracy

- **Bureaucratic Red Tape:** Government offices often contend with complex regulatory frameworks and lengthy approval processes. While these measures ensure transparency and accountability, they can also create inefficiencies and delays in implementing new policies or programs. Employees may experience frustration as they navigate these bureaucratic hurdles, which can impact job satisfaction and productivity.
- **Navigating Change:** Adapting to new technologies, policies, or administrative changes can be challenging in a government setting. Employees may face resistance from colleagues or superiors who are accustomed to traditional methods. Overcoming this resistance requires effective communication and change management strategies to ensure smooth transitions and maintain operational efficiency.

7. Diverse Work Environment

- **Multifaceted Roles:** Government offices employ individuals across a wide range of disciplines, from administrative roles to specialized positions in finance, engineering, healthcare, and education. This diversity fosters a collaborative work environment where different perspectives and expertise contribute to comprehensive problem-solving and innovative solutions.
- **Cultural Competence:** Interacting with colleagues and citizens from diverse cultural backgrounds enhances employees' cultural competence. Understanding and appreciating different cultural perspectives improves the effectiveness of government services, making them more accessible and responsive to the needs of a diverse population.

8. Networking and Community

- **Building Relationships:** Government employees have the opportunity to build extensive networks within their agency and with other departments, non-governmental organizations (NGOs), and community groups. These connections facilitate collaboration on public projects and initiatives, enhancing the overall impact of government programs.
- **Professional Associations:** Many government employees are active in professional associations that advocate for their interests, offer resources, and provide networking opportunities. These associations support career development by offering platforms for sharing best practices, accessing professional development resources, and connecting with peers in the field.

9. Personal Satisfaction

- **Accomplishing Goals:** Government employees often derive personal satisfaction from achieving goals that align with public welfare. Completing projects that improve community infrastructure, enhance educational systems, or provide essential services contributes to a sense of purpose and accomplishment.
- **Public Recognition:** Government employees frequently receive recognition for their contributions, whether through awards, commendations, or public acknowledgment. Such recognition reinforces their commitment to public service and boosts morale, providing positive reinforcement for their efforts and achievements.

Conclusion

Life in government offices presents a complex blend of opportunities and challenges. The stability and structured environment, combined with a strong commitment to public service, create a rewarding career for many. However, employees must navigate bureaucratic processes, adapt to change, and manage diverse work dynamics with resilience and adaptability. While individual experiences vary depending on roles, agency culture, and personal motivations, a career in government often leads to a fulfilling profession with a meaningful impact on society.

Conclusion

As you close the pages of this book, I hope you have found yourself enriched by the detailed recounting of my journey—a journey marked by struggles, perseverance, and eventual triumph. The narrative you have followed delves into various chapters of my life, each filled with its own unique set of challenges and learning experiences. From my early days navigating the complexities of corporate life at L&T Pondicherry to the arduous preparation for competitive exams, and finally to the serene stability of my personal life, this story is a testament to resilience and determination.

Early Challenges at L&T Pondicherry

My professional journey began with my tenure at L&T Pondicherry, a phase characterized by significant cultural and environmental adjustments. Arriving in Pondicherry, I was immediately immersed in a new and unfamiliar food culture. The South Indian culinary traditions, rich in spices and distinct flavors, were a far cry from what I was accustomed to. Adapting to this new cuisine was more than just a matter of taste; it was an essential part of acclimating to my new environment. This culinary transition was compounded by the challenges of working in a demanding corporate atmosphere, where the office environment often felt toxic and stifling.

Navigating office politics, dealing with bureaucratic hurdles, and managing work-related stress tested my patience and adaptability.

The culture at L&T Pondicherry was rigorous and fast-paced, and it was not uncommon to encounter conflicts and friction. This period required me to develop a thicker skin and hone my interpersonal skills to effectively manage these professional hurdles. Despite these challenges, my tenure at L&T Pondicherry was a crucial learning phase, where I learned the importance of resilience and flexibility in the face of adversity.

The Struggles of Competitive Exam Preparation

Transitioning from the corporate world to preparing for competitive exams introduced a new set of challenges. The preparation period was marked by intense dedication and numerous obstacles. I faced extreme weather conditions, studying in a room located on the top floor of my house, which was exposed to both the sweltering heat of summer and the biting cold of winter. The physical discomfort of these conditions made studying a test of endurance and commitment.

During the sweltering summer months, the heat would often become unbearable, making it difficult to focus on my studies. Despite the discomfort, I had to maintain my concentration and motivation. Similarly, the winter brought its own set of challenges, with the cold seeping through and making the study environment harsh and inhospitable. The cold would often lead to distractions and difficulties in maintaining the momentum of my study sessions.

In addition to the physical challenges, I had to contend with emotional and psychological hurdles. The preparation for competitive exams was a grueling process that required not only intellectual effort but also mental fortitude. The pressure to perform well was immense, and there were times when self-doubt crept in. Comments and skepticism from close family and relatives sometimes exacerbated these doubts, making the journey even more daunting. Their concerns, though well-meaning, occasionally undermined my confidence and created moments of hesitation.

Despite these adversities, the process of preparing for and eventually clearing multiple examinations was deeply rewarding. It taught me the value of perseverance and the importance of pushing through even when faced with significant obstacles. The exams were not just academic challenges; they were tests of my resolve and ability to stay focused under pressure.

Achievements and Professional Growth

Through sheer determination and hard work, I successfully cleared several competitive exams for government organizations and public sector undertakings (PSUs). This accomplishment was a culmination of years of effort and sacrifice. The sense of achievement was not merely about passing the exams but about overcoming the myriad challenges that came with the preparation process. It was about proving to myself that I could rise above adversity and succeed in the face of daunting odds.

Clearing these examinations opened doors to new opportunities and a fulfilling career in the public sector. The experience of transitioning from the corporate world to a more stable and purpose-driven career was both gratifying and transformative. It marked the beginning of a new chapter, one that aligned more closely with my personal values and aspirations.

Personal Life and Fulfillment

Today, I am fortunate to enjoy a stable and fulfilling personal life. I am happily married to Mrs. Bineeta Kumari, and we live together with my parents and brother near my hometown in Bihar. This aspect of my life is a source of immense joy and contentment. The support and love of my family have been instrumental in my journey, providing a strong foundation and a sense of belonging.

Living near my hometown has allowed me to stay connected with my roots and maintain a strong bond with my family. This proximity has enriched my life in countless ways, offering both emotional support and a sense of continuity. My family's encouragement and understanding have played a significant role in helping me navigate the challenges and successes of my professional and personal journey.

Reflections and Future Aspirations

As I reflect on my journey, I am filled with a profound sense of gratitude and fulfillment. The path I have traveled has been marked by struggles and triumphs, each contributing to my growth and development. The experiences I have shared—whether they involve overcoming the cultural and environmental challenges at L&T Pondicherry, enduring the rigorous demands of competitive exam preparation, or building a happy and supportive family life—have all shaped who I am today.

I hope that readers have found inspiration in these stories and lessons. Life's journey is rarely smooth, and each of us faces our own set of challenges and hurdles. However, it is through overcoming these obstacles that we grow and find true fulfillment. The key lies in embracing the journey with resilience, determination, and a positive outlook.

To those embarking on their own paths, whether in the corporate world, in academic pursuits, or in personal endeavors, I wish you the best of success. May you find the strength to face challenges head-on and the courage to persevere through difficulties. Remember that every setback is an opportunity for growth, and every challenge you overcome brings you one step closer to achieving your goals.

Thank you for accompanying me on this journey through my experiences. Your engagement with my story is deeply appreciated, and I hope that it has offered you valuable insights and encouragement. As you move forward in your own journey, may you find fulfillment and purpose in every endeavor, and may your efforts lead to meaningful and lasting impacts in your own life and in the lives of others.

Author's Final Message To Readers

"Thank you for embarking on this journey with me. As we conclude this exploration, I hope you find inspiration in the stories and insights shared. Remember, every challenge we face is an opportunity for growth, and every accomplishment is a testament to our resilience. Whether you are navigating a career in government service or pursuing your own path, may these reflections guide you toward finding both fulfillment and purpose. Embrace the journey with an open heart and a determined spirit, knowing that through our collective efforts, we have the power to shape our world and leave a meaningful legacy. Your commitment and passion are the driving forces that create change and make a lasting impact. Keep moving forward with courage and conviction, and let your contributions enrich the lives of those around you."